Iowa Legends
of
BURIED TREASURE

Also by Charlton Grant Laird

"Manuscripts of the *Manuel des Pechiez*," in *Stanford Studies in Language and Literature* (1941)
"Character and Growth of the *Manuel des Pechiez*," in *Traditio* (1946)
Laird's Promptory (1948)
Thunder on the River (1949)
The World Through Literature, editor (1951)
West of the River (1953)
The Miracle of Language (1953)
Modern English Handbook, with Robert M. Gorrell (1953)
Modern English Workbook, with Gorrell (1957)
The Tree of Language, with Helene Laird (1957)
Thinking About Language (1959)
A Course in Modern English, with Gorrell (1960)
English as Language, with Gorrell (1961)
A Basic Course in Modern English, with Gorrell and Raymond J. Pflug (1963)
A Writer's Handbook (1964)
Pickett at Gettysburg, editor (1965)
Casebooks for Objective Writing, general editor (1965-67)
Language in America (1970)
And Gladly Teche (1970)
Words, Words, Words (1970)
Modern English Reader, editor with others (1970,1977)
Webster's New World Thesaurus (1971)
Reading About Language, with Gorrell (1971)
You and Your Language (1973)
Writing Modern English, with Gorrell (1973)

Iowa Legends
of
BURIED TREASURE

by
Charlton Grant Laird

edited by
Stephen K. Hutchinson

Foundation Books
Lincoln, Nebraska

IOWA LEGENDS OF BURIED TREASURE.
Copyright © 1990 by Foundation Books, Inc. All rights reserved.
Printed in the United States of America. No part of this book may be used or reproduced in any manner whatsoever without written permission except in the case of brief quotations embodied in critical articles and reviews. For information address Foundation Books, P.O. Box 29229, Lincoln, NE 68529.

Library of Congress Cataloging-in-Publication Data

Laird, Charlton Grant, 1901-
    Iowa legends of buried treasure / by Charlton Grant Laird : edited by Stephen K. Hutchinson. -- 1st ed.
    p.   cm.
    Thesis (M.A.)--State University of Iowa, 1927.
    Includes bibliographical references (p.   ) and index.
    ISBN 0-934988-23-4 (alk. paper) : $8.95
    1. Iowa--History, Local--Anecdotes. 2. Treasure-trove--Iowa--History--Anecdotes. 3. Legends--Iowa. I. Hutchinson, Stephen K. II. Title.
F621.6.L35 1990
977.7--dc20   90-19777
                                                                                       CIP

First Edition

Most recent printing indicated by the first digit below:
1 2 3 4 5 6 7 8 9 10

The paper used in this publication meets the minimum requirements of American National Standard for Information Sciences - Permanence of Paper for Printed Library Materials, ANSI Z39.48-1984. ∞

Interest in buried treasure is as general as childhood.
-- Charlton Grant Laird

Contents

EDITOR'S PREFACE vii
PREFACE ix
INTRODUCTION: The Nature of Buried Treasure . . . 1

PART 1
TRANSPORTATION TREASURE

1. Four Noble Soldiers 9
2. South of Yellow River 13
3. Billy Nicholson's Pasture 19
4. Buxtom Fell Off the Cliff 23

5. An Awful Heavy Suitcase 27
6. Black Hawk 31
7. A Kid, He Never Forgets 35
8. Whiskey, Gold and Mules 37

9. North Skunk Kettle 39
10. After My Death 43
11. Jack the Fire King 49

PART 2
GOLD THAT FLED VIOLENCE

12. Bushwackers 53
13. The Bellevue War 57
14. Boone River Mound 63
15. Six Hogsheads 65

16. Marble's Gold 67
17. Pest House 69
18. Island Cellar 71
19. Digging Children 73

IOWA LEGENDS OF BURIED TREASURE

20.	Weston Bank Robbers	75
21.	Brush Creek School	77
22.	Precautious as a Preacher	79
23.	Sure as Taillights on a Ford	81
24.	A Woman Laughed	89
25.	Bones and Stones	93
26.	Horse Thieves and Counterfeiters	95
27.	Steamboat Rock	97

PART 3
TREASURES OF QUEER CHARACTERS

28.	No Confidence	105
29.	A Long Slim Box	107
30.	Dust Over Everything	109
31.	Three Brothers	111
32.	They Came and Dug	113
33.	Potato John	115
34.	Old MacDonald	117
35.	Schoolhouse Floor	119
36.	Terribly, Terribly Drunk	121
37.	Dead Ringer	123
38.	Rags	125
39.	Burn the River	129
40.	Dream Tree	131

APPENDIX	135
ENDNOTES	143
BIBLIOGRAPHY	155
INDEX	163

Editor's Preface

ABOUT THE AUTHOR

Charlton Grant Laird (1901-1984) wrote *Iowa Legends of Buried Treasure* in 1927 for his master's thesis at the State University of Iowa.

Laird, who was raised on the family farm near McGregor, IA, had gathered many of the stories while working as a writer for *Wallaces' Farmer*, an Iowa-based weekly agricultural news and entertainment magazine. He solicited stories from family, friends and Iowa readers with the following request from the April 29, 1927, issue of *Wallaces' Farmer*:

> There will be another article in a week or two that will tell more about buried treasure stories in this state. Meanwhile, we would like to ask if our readers know any more yarns of this sort. Did anybody ever bury treasure on your farm or in your neighborhood; or are there any stories that anybody did so? Letters on this subject will be welcome. Five dollars will be given for the best one, and one dollar for each of the others that we use. Give places, dates and sources of information as fully as you can. Keep in mind, too, that the treasure didn't really have to exist for it to provide a good story. If the neighborhood thought there was a treasure, and if folks spent a lot of time digging for it, we will like the account just as well as if somebody did dig up a thousand dollars. The contest closes May 7.

Contest entries were used by Laird in several *Wallaces' Farmer* articles on buried treasures.

Laird continued writing for the magazine as a feature stringer during the late 1920s on subjects ranging from the

IOWA LEGENDS OF BURIED TREASURE

Black Hawk War to stories from the road as he toured the Mississippi Valley in 1929.

The author was born in Nashua, IA, and graduated from McGregor, IA, high school in 1919. He received his B.A. (1925) and his M.A. (1927) from the State University of Iowa. Laird attended Columbia University as a doctoral candidate from 1928-1931 and received his Ph.D. from Stanford University in 1940.

Iowa Legends of Buried Treasure is one of the early works of a prolific writer who loved language. His first published work was a freshman English research paper at the University of Iowa (*Palimpsest*, 1921). He wrote for the *Des Moines Register* and *Tribune* newspapers and organized a news bureau while there. Laird, who described himself as a generalist, authored or edited over 30 books including novels, reference books and textbooks, most notably *The Miracle of Language* and *Language in America*. He was the compiler of *Webster's New World Thesaurus* and published more than a hundred articles, speeches and reviews in publications ranging from *Vanity Fair* to the *Harvard Educational Review*. He is quoted in *The Word: A Look at the Vocabulary of English* as having said, "I would rather write than eat."

EDITORIAL METHOD

The order of the text is the same as the original. .Spelling and grammar have been modernized. Dialectic passages have been modified to facilitate understanding. Additions to the text, such as name changes, are enclosed in brackets. The footnotes have been moved from the body of the text to the endnote section and standardized in form and numbered consecutively instead of by chapter. Approximately 40 footnotes have been deleted or combined. Chapter titles have been changed and map keys added. The bibliography has been restructured and alphabetized and a name index added. Original artwork was no longer available for reproduction.

AKNOWLEDGMENTS

The editor and publisher would like to thank Nancy Laird Hunt, the author's daughter, for allowing Foundation Books to publish *Iowa Legends of Buried Treasure*.

Preface

Legends exist in some plenty, in Iowa. They go back to the earliest settlers. The old tales are still growing and new stories continually appear. The present collection of treasure stories represents an effort to garner the best of these legends and to record their present state of development. The legends here collected touch twenty-five of the ninety-nine counties in the state. Most of the material from the northeast, the southwest and central portions was gathered in person. The stories from the southeast and from the miscellaneous points about the state were happened upon in conversation or brought out through letters. The northwest is poorly represented. The section is younger and probably has fewer legends, but the difficulty of reaching it with any of the means available is certainly significant and perhaps sufficient to account for the paucity of its legends here. Personal investigations were carried on in and around the following towns: Adair, Algona, Ames, Anamosa, Andrew, Atlantic, Bellevue, Cedar Rapids, Council Bluffs, Des Moines, Dunreath, Eddyville, Eldora, Giard, Iowa City, McGregor, Maquoketa, New Albin, Spirit Lake, Rising Sun, State Center, Steamboat Rock, Thurman, Waukon, Waukon Junction. In all cases an effort was made to locate the most likely tale tellers and to put them at their ease. They were encouraged to tell the story freely, but without embellishments of their own. Some of the letters were obtained by personal solicitation and the rest through the offer of one five-dollar prize by *Wallaces' Farmer* and an additional dollar for each letter published. It was thought that such reward could scarcely encourage prevarication.

Most of the stories are too young to support many branches and little surety can be offered for the folk origin of any of the versions. The legend of McGregor Gold is given here in five versions, which show some variation. It might be noted that

IOWA LEGENDS OF BURIED TREASURE

the transportation of money near forts is the characteristic common to these stories, and that most of the narrators insist upon one or more deaths. Three of the assaults were credited to Indians. In all but one of the variations, the money was buried intentionally and two of the sites are said to be described in documents. In four of the legends the money was being transported between forts and by varying numbers of men. In no two of the stories do the routes of travel coincide.

Of the hazards of transporting money, the most frequently traveled highway was the old military road between Forts Crawford and Atkinson. A conjecture that this trail gave birth to the original story would seem to be borne out.

With the Missouri River legends, where various vessels sank in a half dozen places and from several causes, agreement is limited to the accidental wrecking of a boat with precious cargo.

It is notable in Iowa that good legends do not exist without good reconteurs and the good storytellers seemingly never want for a story. Some of the legendarians quoted here could supply a tale on almost any subject and others interviewed were hopelessly barren.

None of the legendarians are dull. Some have no question that the legislature would readily appropriate $100,000 to an Indian for a bit of rascality, or that a doddering old man would lug two or three hundred pounds of gold to the top of a three-hundred-foot bluff and expect to tramp fifty miles through the woods and prairies with it. None conclude the $80,000 would garrison, not one fort for a year, but all of the forts in the northwest for a considerable period. But the ability to vision, retain, organize and tell even a simple story demands appreciation of incident, control over the course of events and some facility of expression.

Interest in buried treasure is as general as childhood. Gold has always been close to the heart of romance. That Henry James objected to hunting buried treasure would probably be forgotten had he not been mentioned by Robert Louis Stevenson. In "A Humble Remonstrance," Stevenson said, "There never was a child (unless Master James) but has hunted gold, and been a pirate, and a military commander and a bandit of the mountains."

Perhaps three fourths of the material was gathered in personal interviews. Stories from good narrators are told as

Preface

by a single legendarian, usually unaided by questions. Where there was no agreement as to the story, or where no narrator proved capable of weaving the threads, existing strands have been wound together. Without too thoroughly disrupting the sequence of stories, I have made an effort to indicate those narrators and the parts of their tales that required questions. Storytellers who were not too rambling have been included entire, and where tact forbade writing during the interview, the complete conversation was set down at the earliest opportunity, usually within the hour and always during the day. Actual names are omitted only where their inclusion would be embarrassing or libelous.

The remaining material came from letters submitted in contests conducted by Laura Lou Brookman in *The Des Moines Register* and by Donald R. Murphy in *Wallaces' Farmer*. This type of material is designated as it appears.

Suggestions for searches came from friends, student groups, county histories, newspaper files and blind gropings in communities known to look back upon a colorful past. Promising legends were pursued in investigations touching twenty-five. counties scattered over the state. The wealth of material in these communities encourages the belief that stories presented here include but a small part of existing legend and lore, although the regularity with which the several motifs appeared throughout the investigation would suggest that the tales are fairly representative.

Friends and even bare acquaintances have been at pains to make material available. To them much is due. Especial credit should be accorded Professor Edwin Fort Piper for his suggestions both as folklorist and critic.

IOWA LEGENDS OF BURIED TREASURE

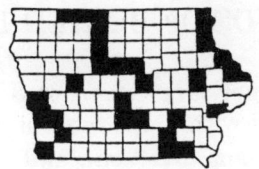

Introduction

Romance oft owes allegiance to wealth, and to many of the world's best tales, treasure troves are sovereign. Sons of woodcutters acquire kings' daughters and kings' acres. Patch-eyed pirates stoutly refuse to scuttle ships in palm-lined southern seas, unless there are doubloons in profusion. Fabulous wealth, hidden wealth and, especially, mysterious wealth, even though legendary, has fired men's minds and enlisted folklore.

First troves entrenched themselves before any wealth appeared above ground. North American Indians lead explorers over long trails to their deaths. The Inca nation so staggered under wealth that actual and legendary treasures brought about its ruin.[1]

Primitive imagination supplied fairies and goblins with gold.

Riches were succeeded to; conquerors only were heroes and gold supply was not to be impugned.[2]

Civilization was not old, however, before definite provision was made for buried wealth. Clovis scattered "The Great Treasure of Guordon" over all France, as a peasant's discovery of a strange plate amply demonstrates.[3] The Moors sowed it so thickly in Spain that the men of Don Alonzo de Aquilar gave over the pursuit of shrieking Moorish beauties to cast their arms aside and load themselves with plunder and met thus their death.[4] The Master Treasure is not sufficiently revealed in the mystic letters, "NEMO," carved upon the tomb of an abbot.[5] In Cornwall[6] Gerennius, a mythical king, lies buried in his golden boat, his finger bones still lying over the handles of his silver oars and the gold and jewels of his crown circling his mouldy skull.[7] About him every menhir has its treasure, but providential storms guard them from the acquisitive. Such scatterings of gold are but pocket money to

IOWA LEGENDS OF BURIED TREASURE

the treasures of the Americas. Governor Boabdilla, during the Sixteenth Century, took with him a table of pure gold reputed to weigh 360,000 castellanos (over one and one half tons).[8] He went, on the occasion, to the bottom of the sea at the east end of his island, Hispaniola. Quesada, hunting the famed El Dorado, was disappointed and came away with a pittance of gold, a heap only high enough that "a rider on horseback might hide behind it."[9] The ransom for Atahaulpa, head Inca of Peru, was golden vessels to fill a room twenty-two by seventeen feet to the depth of nine feet.[10] In Central America native Indians excavated a vault, "where they piled up countless bars of virgin gold." American soldiers are digging the island of Luzon into fertility if they are not civilizing the natives, for Drake buried money there, and all the deltas of the Mississippi River cannot embed the gold that Jean Lafitte left along the Gulf.[11] Vast sums involved in the Mexican War were buried in Texas[12] and several chests of French gold were planted by one Claireaux on Grand Island in the Niagara River.[13] Of course the gold has been sought, but usually with indifferent success. It is said that more than $100,000 spent plumbing Oak Island, Nova Scotia, has produced constant encouragement, but no treasure.[14] In treasure digging, mention should be made of the poet who arrived at Worms, Germany, equipped with a volume of Wagner, the price of a skiff and a determination to find the gold of the Nibelungs.[15]

In Iowa, treasure legends have profited from at least three encouragements: the uncertainty of transportation, the fear of violence, and the interest in queer characters. In fact, violence and the transportation of money in these legends are so allied that the one is seldom found without the other. Even in a tale like that of the old man who stopped at the government barn in Clayton County, the apparently simple transportation motif is doubtless complicated by two frontier forts. In the legend at Eddyville one wonders whether the murder of Bill Gunton or flight from the body brought about the burial of his $30,000.

Tales gathered here are only a small portion of existing lore. During interviewing for one story, I've often found other tales. One half day of interviewing traces of three distinct treasure legends, I found one developed sufficiently to be included here and vestiges of more than one tale. Prejudice or

Introduction

comfort makes some sections hostile, but communities with encouraging home conditions and without treasure legends would seem rare.

Tales grew healthily along the northern course of the Mississippi River. The first Iowa explorers and settlers landed here were followed by the first Iowa prosperity. All this meant buried treasure, but money was transported at a time when safety was providential and when ingenuity and credulity were the only checks upon rumor. Forts, Indian battle grounds, bandit bands and vigilantes bordered the river.

River life was hard and dangerous, but it was also gay and it paid. Mines and saw mills brought a flow of money. Trade from the agricultural lands to the west stirred it in flux and murder kept it in danger. Men of imagination quickened river bluff life.

But, with the coming of rail transportation, trade that had followed the rivers north and south turned east and west. As they lost trade, river towns shrank, and even the flood of immigration helped little. River land was too rugged to appeal to farmers. Those who were there, stayed. Why not? There were few to disturb what they had. They had their memories of a colorful past and stories to retell.

Treasure tales readily mold toward a pattern. Money appears, accompanied by questionable characters. Hazard in transportation throws the money into receptive and illegitimate hands. Fear may urge honest people to consign their wealth to earth. Gold-laden rogues in haste bury gold before the hounds catch them. Even whim and family quarrels induce interment of treasure.

Once gold is underground, any and all means are called upon to keep it there forever if possible, but certainly until the original owner is elsewhere. Frequently he who planted the gold is killed as an incident to the treasure burying. If he lives he loses his memory or is overtaken by old age before he can return.

Maps and charts get lost, or were drawn in such haste and awkwardness, and are not to scale, so are subject to wide interpretation. If the treasure lies under a flat rock, can a four-foot by two-foot boulder, thick in the middle, be called flat? How big is a big tree? Would a stump have been a big tree fifty years ago? If the gold lies along Beaver River, shall we

IOWA LEGENDS OF BURIED TREASURE

hunt the Big Beaver or was there a slight mistake that diverted the story from Kiever River? How high must dirt be heaped to become a hill? If the money hides "in the third grove on the north bank of the river" do you count the groves on the south side of the river for the first two and how many trees does it take to make a grove anyway? When treasure hunters decide these and more they still find that gullies have intervened to make paced distances shift with erosion, that trees have been cut, stumps grubbed and rocks herded into fences, that rivers have changed their courses and dried up entirely, that islands have been washed away. Thus it is perhaps not surprising if money can little more be enticed from under ground than a rat can be challenged from its hole, and should it ever stray to the surface guardian ghosts or the devil himself may protect it.[16] Where there is no murder or where the dead guardian is peaceable or even helpful, discovery is possible. Divining rods are a great aid in locating gold and troves are sometimes coquettish enough to attract attention to themselves,[17] but even so, discoveries are rare and not always happy.

A chronology of legends would be difficult, but it may be valuable to note that some events have encouraged them. The Black Hawk War and the soldier activity, 1828-32, started many stories. Earlier Indian troubles fathered stories in the East, but after tribal departure from the Mississippi River the Frontier moved rapidly west until the border was given another emphasis by the Spirit Lake massacre in 1857. Then the Civil War and its Unionist-Copperhead dissentions fostered instability[18] and motivated pioneers to bury bullion. Between these two dates the operations of bandit gangs were a fluctuating prod to caution and in the latter part of the century the James brothers were perhaps the strongest excitant.[19]

Fabulous legends do not necessarily presuppose great treasure. Washington Irving has noted "that the stories of treasure buried by the Moors which prevail throughout Spain are the most current among the poorest people. It is thus kind nature consoles with shadows for the want of substantials."[20] Legends would seem to be the homely literature of escape. The urge that poverty has given Iowa tales leads one to believe that the actual pleasure of telling treasure legends and of hunting mysterious and lost things, coupled with hope, credulity and ethnocentrism, has been responsible for the preservation and

Introduction

the growth of legends. Of course, the whole is abetted by bad memories and active imaginations.

However, legendarians as a class attempt honesty, accuracy and skepticism. They include sober, educated folk who pride themselves on the practical virtues. They are characterized not by poverty, but by the fullness of their lives and by their innate joy in telling a story well.

In Iowa it is perhaps misleading to say that "many a treasure legend has originated in motives as innocent as those of Uncle Remus,"[21] but Iowa tales certainly owe much of their ornament to good fellowship. If the situation demands a tale, why let cold reason kill it?

Buried treasure fosters the strange, the mysterious and possibly happy ending. Over half of a Des Moines freshman high school composition class, permitted for the first time to write stories after their hearts, produced tales of hidden valuables, most of them buried. Even adults who would never go treasure hunting, are glad to pass on necessary information.[22] Such readiness warms the teller and the tale.

Quite as potent is the desire on the part of the narrator to encourage his own hope, to retain the possibility of finding unexpected treasure.[23] In a world in which few are financially satisfied and in which most indulge rather more of the prerequisite to competence than is their pleasure, men readily dream of mythical wealth. Probably no story teller can delight others without himself coming closer to conviction in his tale, and such conviction may provide his greatest pleasure in the telling. While he can believe that buried money is charted and yet undug, while he can trust that others have found such treasure, and while he can know more than others of any particular buried wealth and thus retain more chance of finding it, he has drawn most of a circle whose completion would please him mightily. Such an interest livens the tongue of the narrator and clears the ear of him who listens.[24]

Buried treasure and its adjuncts have often within themselves means of self-perpetuation. Gold is not long separated from blood, nor blood from gold. The stories connected with buried treasure are frequently in themselves racy enough to guarantee re-telling. Legends, like other commodities, profit from a lively trade. Much that has been preserved is apparently the accretion upon an incident

5

powerful enough to overcome the imaginations of those who were spatially close to it. Given intense interest in a situation, connected even rather remotely with money or an excuse to bury it, one may expect with moderate confidence that buried treasure angles will develop. As the story is repeated in subsequent years, sodden intellects present but the staff of the tale while the more productive find legend. They garner where they may, and, grateful for celestial bounty, ignore the hierarchy of fact.

These stories served as accretion points for lore. Some of the stories given here are still essentially historical; others give little trace of an ancestor.

Let us turn to the legends. However they may appear here, they affected me as I gathered them as being honest, living and significant, as having within them the vitality of collective creation.

Part 1
TRANSPORTATION TREASURE

Oh, the hazards of travel by land or water. Waterways were riotous, were frontiers, highways and havens. Gold sifted down their boiling currents and in flood times was deposited all along the banks. Rascals could be lords among transients and travelers were profitable subjects. The surge of frontier life, the threat of Indian uprisings, the glamour and graft of military law did little to sanctify early river towns. The floes of land people and water people met at the crooked river's edge. Stagecoaches mired, steamboats burned, grounded, or exploded when a racing captain removed a bothersome pop-off valve. While money-laden passengers blew to eternity, their treasures bore fruit in lore and legend.

IOWA LEGENDS OF BURIED TREASURE

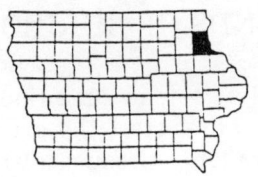

1.
Four Noble Soldiers
McGregor Gold
Clayton County

At its crossing from Minnesota, the Mississippi River flows past the untold plunder of Black Hawk and where the Des Moines River meets it at the edge of Missouri, the treasure cache of the Banditti of the Prairies once nestled in a hanging valley. The northern hills approach three hundred feet in height, timber-crested and bold with sheer rock faces that frown down upon the river. Square, shouldering bluffs they are that thrust themselves toward the river and brood eternally. At their feet, shrunken towns squat like old men in the sun and babble of those days the river was hot with young blood. There are heaps of stones and rotted piling, left as in memories. Old maps show a name and old river men tell a tale for each of these spots, but the towns were born of river traffic. Theirs was a race out of time.

No contraceptive could keep such a land from bearing treasure legends. Some thirty-five miles south of the border, where the Wisconsin River swerves from the east and is shunted south by the original Pike's Peak, Marquette first set foot on Iowa soil.

McGregor, a few miles north, is one of the oldest towns in Iowa, only slightly antedated by Prairie du Chien across the river in Wisconsin. Prairie du Chien sits on bottom land nearly a mile wide and fronts into a labyrinth of islands and sloughs. The Iowa bluffs bathe their feet in the river and force McGregor back into a pocket-like valley.

Such it must have been in 1830 when commanding officer Col. Zachary Taylor stamped among the up-ended logs that were officially termed, Fort Crawford.[25] There was reason for his stamping. With a slender garrison, he was expected,

IOWA LEGENDS OF BURIED TREASURE

officially if dubiously, to fend ambitious savages from the northwestern frontier, to protect the priceless American lives of rascally Indian traders, to educate the aborigines and to develop the country.

One version of Taylor's predicament was provided by the *Crawford County Press*, and reprinted in the *North Iowa Times*, July 20, 1905, page one. Preceding the passage are two paragraphs on the imminence of Black Hawk's war. The threat became operative in 1832.

"One day in 1830, four bags of gold were received at the fort, to be used in payment of the United States soldiers on duty at the stockade. The gold was in coins of large denomination, and the amount of the consignment reached to $890,000.[26] This was the largest amount of coin ever shipped to a western point, and the utmost secrecy attended its shipment and its care after it had reached its destination. Colonel Taylor, when apprised of its arrival, took all possible pains for its safe keeping until such a time as the Indians could again be driven away.

"Calling together the command, he chose from the men four of the bravest and most trustworthy of them, and after informing them of the importance of the mission with which he was about to intrust them, he gave them each a bag of gold with instructions to carry it to a safe place which he should select, and there hide it from the eyes of the Indians. An attack being feared at any moment, as well as the loss of the gold, the men went their way, at once with the gold in their possession.

"Hardly had they left the stockade when a well-planned attack was made and after the repulse many of the brave defenders were found dead in their tracks. The battles and the skirmishes were kept up for many days in search of the four men to whom had been intrusted the bags of gold. After three or four days of strict search, the bodies of the men were found, stark and dead.

"Not the smallest suggestion of the gold could be found about the place where the men had lost their lives in the defense of their trust, but after a thorough search, one of the members of the party was rewarded by finding a scrap of paper near the body of one of the men (known) as Mercierre. Upon this scrap of paper was scrawled the intelligence that the money had been buried in the highest point across from the place where they were found. It is supposed that the poor fellow upon finding that his minutes were numbered hastily wrote the few words on

Four Noble Soldiers

the bit of paper and throwing it in the bushes in the hope that his comrades would find it, he bravely met his death.

"At the close of the hardest of the fighting, parties were sent in search of the money, but the four bags were never found. The men had evidently fulfilled their trust carefully and as a result they buried the money so well that not the slightest sign of disturbance of the soil could be found at any place about the bluff.

"Hundreds of people have worked by the day in an effort to locate a trace of the thousands of dollars buried in the lonely bluff, but all efforts have been unavailing and the gold yet lies where it was buried by the brave fellows who took their lives in hand to protect the earnings of their fellow soldiers."[27]

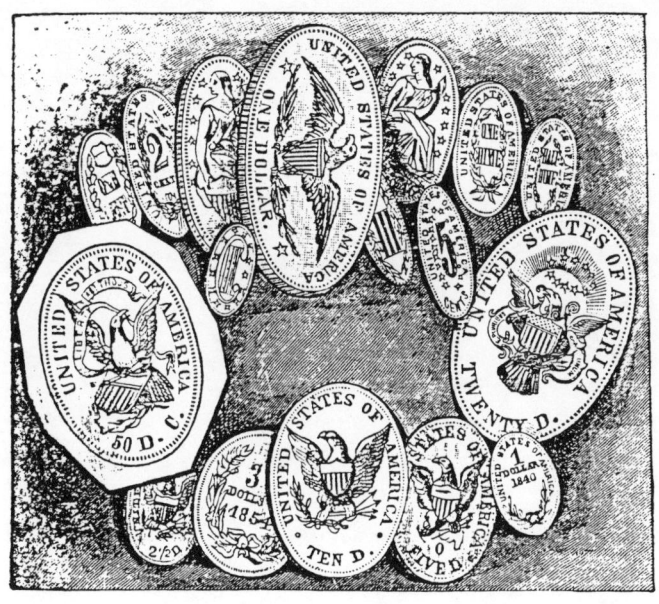

IOWA LEGENDS OF BURIED TREASURE

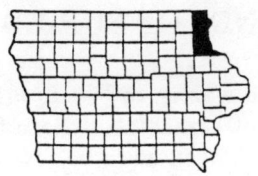

2.
South of Yellow River
McGregor Gold
Clayton and Allamakee Counties

I first heard the story from my mother. I had asked for some trinket or other and she postponed me by saying, "until we find the gold buried on the hill." At once I forgot my trinket campaign, as she doubtless suspected I would, and listened while she told the story. Many times afterward our entire family speculated good humoredly on the change such a find would have on our fortune. I believe they enjoyed the story as much as I did.

Mrs. J. G. Laird, now nearly seventy, lives near Waukon Junction. I recently asked her to retell the story.

"Of course, we never took much stock in it ourselves," Mrs. Laird said, "but they told your father about it even before he bought the place. We didn't go 'round hunting for it--now let me see--they talked quite a bit about it. There were these men. I think there were four of them. They had the money and were bringing it from some fort, Crawford? Crawford. It would be Crawford, wouldn't it, and they were going to pay the soldiers at some fort out west, Fort Atkinson, I believe. They came up that old military road and then they were chased by somebody, was it Indians or somebody disguised as Indians? They were chased, let's see, and they thought they were going to lose the money so they buried it and I think they were all killed, or did they get away? Anyway, they left a document telling where to find the gold. I said--it was written in French, I know because it was Mrs. K. that first told me the story. She was French, or French extraction and could read French. She had seen the

IOWA LEGENDS OF BURIED TREASURE

document, now where was it, in Washington? I think. It was in French and was put someplace where those who could read French could see it. There were so few then who could read anything but French, and it told, so many feet from a certain tree, you know. Some said the money was buried on the first bluff from the old road. That would be the one south of Yellow River, and some said the second bluff. That would be ours. There was $80,000 and they had equal parts. I don't remember just how the message was saved so that people saw it. Perhaps one of them wasn't killed, or they found it on a body or they stuck it up somewhere.

"My sister, Marjorie, was of the impression that the money was buried in four lots of $20,000 each and my older brother, Burton, was sure he had heard the directions, "under a flat stone beneath an oak tree on the highest bluff directly across from Fort Crawford."[28]

Mrs. R. L. Brown, a farm woman approaching middle age, formerly lived on the bluff north of Yellow River. I have the following from her, dated at Waukon Junction: "I don't know much more about the Yellow River treasure, I'm sure than the rest of you, but Mrs. Vera K-- of McGregor, whose husband owned the launch 'Rustler' and rustled other things than picnic parties and bridal parties, was quite literary in a way. She wrote for the local papers, etc., and was considered quite a 'joke' locally because she thought she could write a story anybody would want to read. However, she was at that time on the editorial staff of *'Pictorial Review,' 'Little Folks,' 'American Boy,'* and *'Munsey.'* She painted quite nicely-- even sold some originals of the Mississippi to eastern magazines for covers. I know that is so for she had the magazines at the house with them on and they were signed 'Waulter Scott,' the name she used for all literary and art work. She both read and wrote French and talked it, I guess. The record left of the treasure was written in French and she had a chance not only to see but have it in her possession long enough to translate. She said after that she knew we owned the right point.

"I never saw her to talk with her after I was married [1908]. Soon after that her husband went to work for 'Uncle Sam' and she with her little three-year-old Vera K-- went to live with a married daughter in Mason City.

South of Yellow River

"I believe the record was at the Dubuque County courthouse, but it may have been the public library of Dubuque. Anyway, she went and read it."

The tale thus centers about the military road that clambers west from the river, across surly bluffs and on into the prairie to where the town, Fort Atkinson, now stands. Its eastern termination is a narrow gorge ending in a meagre, rock-piled delta. Boats landed here, and here by 1840 was an odor of civilization, a so-called Nezeka,[29] promoted by H. L. Dousman of Prairie du Chien. Supplies destined for Fort Atkinson were ferried here and hauled west.

"Uncle Larry" Jennings and "Aunt Fron," 84 and 80 years of age respectively, are now retired and living in McGregor, but for half a century their home stood just where the old military road broke onto the hill top. To them I went.

"I don't know that I can tell you much," cautioned Uncle Larry. "The money is supposed to be buried on my bluff, but we don't neither of us really know nothin' about it--only what we heard. It was before our time. The story is that it all happened about when they expected a break among the Indians anyway. When was that, Ma, do you remember? Well, it was when this was all woods, anyway. You see, my father was a cooper and a man in Prairie wanted him to get out some wagon timber over here. He came over and then he found he didn't have the rights to it, so he went to farmin' what he could. They had one team of oxen and that was traded around the neighborhood.

"The old military road come right up over the hill east of our place. There was a big barn and a house down at the foot of it when we come."

"I remember just as well running down that hill when I was a girl," Aunt Fron interposed. "It was a good dug road."

"They was coming up that hill with the gold," Uncle Larry went on, "gold for the soldiers--$80,000 of it, for the men at Fort Atkinson. Now how was it they come to bury that before they was attacked?"

"They had word they was going to be attacked," said Aunt Fron, "and they buried the money. They either buried it just before they got to the top of the hill or just after they got there. Buried it in a brass kettle.[30]

IOWA LEGENDS OF BURIED TREASURE

"Old Mis' Bowlder found a twenty-dollar gold piece," said Aunt Fron. "She found it just below that tree in the turn of the road just below my place."

"That was where they used to do all their tradin'," Uncle Larry said.

"No, it wasn't," said Aunt Fron. "That was farther down." As a child I turned over flat stones until I raised blisters, but the practice was not restricted to children. One McGregor business man, a municipal official and Sunday School superintendent, hired a laborer to dig for the money. Willis Bickel, who owns the bluff north of McGregor, told me that treasure hunters had dug up his permanent surveying marks, iron pegs that he had sunk below the frost line.

Joseph Shafer, superintendent of The State Historical Society of Wisconsin, wrote me under the date of January 13: "The result of the promulgation of this legend at Prairie du Chien was that so much digging occurred around the ruins of old Fort Crawford as to sensibly aid in the demolition of those ruins."

The Wisconsin state park south of Prairie du Chien contains "Treasure Cave," and commemorates thus a twist to the tale that brings the beleaguered soldiers to it.

Point Anne, south of McGregor, has received the gold one or more times. From my childhood in the territory I should not hesitate to declare that every section of land for ten miles along the Iowa side of the river has provided that $80,000 several habitats.

Even if one were to accept any single set of directions, they remain pleasantly resourceful. Consider my brother's "under a flat stone beneath an oak tree on the highest bluff directly across from Fort Crawford." The river here is two miles from bluff to bluff, and it curves so that Prairie du Chien is within a large arc having a straight line tangent to it. Thus the gazer from any hill for miles along the Iowa bank can see, with sufficient imagination and proprietary pride, old Fort Crawford directly opposite him. All would not agree that the tallest hills are those across from the fort, but the other details are accurate. They must be, and therein lies further confusion. Bluff crests are all timbered. The trees are all deciduous and oaks are the most frequent. Upper ledges are lime rock. Most of the chips are large and all of them are flat. In short, the river is lined with high hills across from Fort

South of Yellow River

Crawford, each of which is covered with oak trees with large flat rocks about their roots. There are still many likely, unprobed spots, and chances improve.

Many explain the failure of these hunts, but there are also those who attribute disappointment to the earlier success of Dousman.[31] Mrs. Daniel Davis of McGregor, now about seventy-five years of age, lived at Nezeka in her girlhood and tells me that her mother was there at the time of the abduction.

"Don't you ever think that money's buried up on that bluff. Yes, it was buried up there alright, but old Dousman got that money. That's who got it. My mother seen him do it. That's what he built his hotel with.[32] What else would he build it with? He wasn't nothing but an ordinary old trader before he stole that money and took on airs. Don't you go wasting your time digging for that money, now. My mother seen him when he hauled that money across the river on the ice in a bob-sled. The soldiers that was killed on the bluff--the Indians killed and scalped 'em. The soldiers had buried the money, $80,000 in gold, on top of the bluff. Old Dousman was up to some of his crooked business. It was just like him. He couldn't lie straight in bed, and he found out where that money was hid. Like as not he had some of his Indian relatives find it. He married an old squaw to git the Indians' money, you knew that, didn't you? Maybe he suspicioned they was money being sent and got his Indian friends to kill the soldiers. He'd do that. Then he dug up the money wherever they had secretted it.

My mother seen Old Dousman bring the gold down the hill and put it in a sled covered with robes. No, indeed, she didn't see the gold. Old Dousman was too smart for that. He had it all disguised over with blankets. He never knew my mother seen him. She watched him and his henchmans out the window and they was in such a hurry they didn't look around much. They pertended like they'd been hunting or something and the gold was in the carcass. But it wasn't. You can mark that. Old Dousman didn't go shooting in the dead of winter. His pesky old Indian relatives did his hunting for him. If you want to find that gold, you go over to Prairie. That's where that gold went to."

IOWA LEGENDS OF BURIED TREASURE

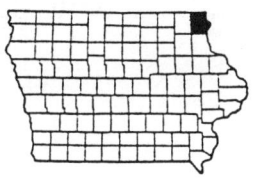

3.
Billy Nickolson's Pasture
McGregor Gold
Allamakee County

The story was told me by Orley Le Hew, a sawyer now some fifty-five years of age, living a mile southeast of Waukon Junction.

"Yes, I know the money was found. Oh, I don't exactly know it, but it looks mighty queer to me if it wasn't, and I can tell you the man that found it.
"As I heard it, they was two fellers comin' with money to pay off soldiers. They was sixty to a hundred thousan' dollars. They was goin' to Fort Crawford to pay off the Indian fighters. They was carryin' this money with 'em and they had two Indian guides. Now, where'd they come from? Some fort in Minnesoty. Well, no matter. They just got down into Yeller River bottoms and they was shot. But, that's ahead 'n the story.
"A lot of folks thinks that money wasn't down in there, but they don't know what I know. They thinks it ought to be up along the ridge where the road runs, but they don't know they us't to be a old Indian trail right down through Billy Nickolson's pasture and down through Sixteen and up the Dousman Coolie.
"The white men was follered. Some said it was for the gold the Indians 'd got wind of and some that they was follered for a perticular reason--Orville, you go on out to your mother like a good boy. Go on now--he'd wronged a woman, a young 'Jibway squaw up in the copper country and her brothers was a doggin' him. Some says the Indian guides was trying to perteck him. Some say not. But when they git down in the

IOWA LEGENDS OF BURIED TREASURE

Yeller River bottoms, they cleared out kite and kaboodle and the whites seed they was in for it.

"They figgered around and they calclated they better bury the gold and git. They took their camp kettle and buried it at the foot of a big maple tree with the gold in it and left markings and blazings to find her with. Purty soon they was ambrushed and shot and when (sheriff's) posses went out to look for 'em, they found their bodies and a note telling where the money was. That's how they knowed it was Indians. The Redskins had taken their knives and weapons and clothes, but they'd left the paper with some other debreez that'd come out of the pockets.

"That's what I heard, as a feller will, and now comes what I know. A young kid was grubbin' out about six mile south of Sixteen, no, southeast it'd be. He was workin' for a rich old codger and this neighbor boy was helpin' him, grub out a big stump. One day they swung a mattock into some metal and dug out a big iron kettle. They couldn't lift it nohow, but rolled it out. The cover was rusted tight. This older feller knew which side his bread was buttered on. I knew him. I was workin' on a farm at the time. It must have been about 1904 or 1905, early spring. He sent the kid up to the house after a pinch bar sayin' he couldn't get the lid off. The kid came back with the bar and the kettle was gone.

"The old codger said he'd got the lid open, but it was empty and for the kid to git to work.

"The kid thought that was kinda funny, but he was just a kid and not too smart at that and the other feller was a man. He told it to his daddy and they was some talk at the time, but this young feller--his name was Jake, I believe--was an awful feller for jollyin'.

"Come fall, this older feller moved out to Coloraddy. Nobody heard nothin' for some years.

"But Jake kep' a talkin' about a man not bein' able to get a start in this damn country--just a half-witted kid growed up and not gettin' nowhere.

"Then Jake got a letter from the old codger sayin' if he'd come to Coloraddy he'd give him a start. He went out there and Jake bought him a quarter section. Built him a house and buildings as nice as you please and stocked out with every thing a man'd want. I know fellers that has seen the place, and they all said they wan't a better.

Billy Nicholson's Pasture

"I allers figgered he found that kettle a' gold and he figgered if he told folks the guv'ment 'd git it, so he jest kep' it secret and made it up to the kid. I know fellers that has throwed it up to him jest for cur'osity, and he'd only laugh at 'em. He's got relations livin' up by Waterville and when I was workin' alongside of him one time in thrashin' time, I asked him jest like that. He looked queer like, but he never answered me aye, yes, no, go-to-hell, or nuthin!"[33]

IOWA LEGENDS OF BURIED TREASURE

4.
Buxtom Fell Off the Cliff
McGregor Gold
Clayton and Allamakee Counties

There are at least two parts to the legend. The first of those given here was told by Mr. and Mrs. Charlie Carney and their son Ted. They are aged about 55, 50 and 16 respectively and make their living by raising ginseng on their forty acres two miles west of Waukon Junction and by hunting it through the surrounding woods.

The Carneys live in a paper covered shack inserted in the side of their property. When I arrived about six o'clock one morning Charlie was as yet without either his breakfast or his shoes. Mrs. Carney worked at a cook stove in the corner during our talk.

They greeted me as the son of an old friend and talked readily. He referred to himself as "The Old Man."

"Yep," said Mr. Carney, "I know where that guv'ment money is. But we couldn't get to it without an arryplane. Now, what I'm wonderin' is, would they be liable to anything come out a' this story if I told you? I told a few felluhs 'bout the money, but I ain't never told nobody but the missus where she lay. I know where to git it, but I can't git it alone. Ef you wrote that fur a piece in the paper, now, I wonder if I'd git some help on it?"

I admitted that most things are possible.

"Ya see, I been all over those hills. I ain't 'fraid a' nothin an' I goes all over these hills. Some places I hadn't orter. Now, I knowed about this gold fur a great piece, an' I been a thinkin' about it an' that's one reason I come back down here, to find that gold. I spent most of last summer an' the summer before an' I been in every cave along the river 'cept one an' that's the one you can't git to without the arryplane. An' that's where the gold lays.

"Ya see I got special reason for knowin' jest where to find that gold. I was the man that found Old Buxtom where he lay to the foot of that bluff fur clean two year before he was found."

"It's jest a year an' nine months," Mrs. Carney corrected.

"That's nigh two year. Well, there he lay. They was somethin' funny about that bluff. Four hundred feet high she was to the top. And that man fell that four hundred feet and they wa'n't a broken bone in his body, not narry. An' the man that helped me get him out, near got bit of a rattlesnake. They was two on one side of him an' two to t'other an' I yelled to him to jump to the rock above an' he done it. That saved him. Well, Old Buxtom might of got rattlesnake bit, too, cuz it seems kind a' funny they wa'n't no bones broke an' him fallin' four hunderd feet.

"But if he did, where was his gold-headed cane? That was the puzzler. I looked apiece fur that cane. I follered up along the path he must a' climbed an' he must a' gone right over the peak. Right down a' that peak was a narrer bencht like, and I figgered that the cane bein' heavy of its gold head must have just nacherly fell straighter an' hit that little bencht like.

"Well, I got to thinkin', and you know, that place where Old Buxtom fell off'n the clift, right up to Johnson's Port [Johnsonport], that was the very place the old man went what had that guv'ment gold. Some says as it was in coin, sixty thousand I think I heard in a keg. But I allus figgered it must a been nuggets and gold, else why'd they carry it in a keg? How did they pay the soldiers anyhow, in coin or dust? You see this old man had the gold to pay all them forts west a' here-- where he was goin'. Ma?"

Ma thought there were quite enough forts to which he might be going.

"I know," said Carney, "they was goin' down to McDowell's."

"Course! Course! To the Mission."

"Yeah, that mission or fort or whatever it was and they was more on west. Ya see, he went up that same place and I allus figured he fell off just where Old Buxtom did or maybe the robbers got him. I 'nquired 'round quiet like of Old

Buxtom Fell Off the Cliff

Boardmann and McGowan and some of the old ones an' they said they was a robbers' cave there. I tried all summer to git down in there and I couldn't make it. Seems like a man used to could git down from the top, but it'd caved in both ways. The only way a man'd git there now is with a arryplane like I told you, and I don't s'pose he could land that, could he?"

I suggested a rope.

"Well, yes, a man might make it if he had the sand, right down that rock face. Now, I ain't 'fraid a' nothin'; I'd do it if I's sure a' man on top. As I say, I was scoutin' 'round there below where Old Buxtom fell an' where the cave has the money in it is, and what did I find gleamin' out a' the leaves but a lump a' gold 'bout the size of a wald nut an' I went to pawing 'round an' there was another, right nigh the first. I sent that gold away to have it tested an' the feller tested it said it was Californy gold. You know them fellers tests it can tell jest where gold come from. Course, it might have been jest dropped by some miner back from Californy, but if that was part of the guv'ment gold, the rest 'd be on that bencht.

"Now they was 'nother thing. That was when I was a young feller, not more'n twenty-two or three. That's where I found that rod. You remember, Ma."

"Yes," said Mrs. Carney, "and Mary told about that, too. But you were older 'n that. You were clost thirty."

"No, I wasn't. I was. . . ."

"Why, Mary was born. . . ."

In the ensuing pause after discussing dates, Carney went on. "Anyhow, I come home an' I says to the woman, 'I'm goin' out to the p'int. I want to see how the old Mississippi looks an' I might see some sang [ginseng]. Mary was a little tot then an' took her along with me an' left her by a big fallen down oak tree. The stump was holler, an' she, kid-fashion, pawed all that soft rotten stuff outa there, you see, an' a piece of iron like was layin' in the ground, buggered a little, but thins I, 'I'll see what you are', an' I picks it up.

"Well, when I goes to pick it up I see it was fastened down. But I pulled a little an' out I drawed that rod. It was about four foot long. I was going' to keep it fur a walkin' stick, then I jest stuck it back in the ground. I looked for that rod time an' time again since, but I never located that stump but it was right up above this cave at Johnson's Port. Do you reckon a feller'd git a pitcher from the river?

IOWA LEGENDS OF BURIED TREASURE

I mentioned telescopic cameras and added a warning about light.

"Sun shines in there bright about seven of a morning. I honestly believe that money's in that cave."

This rather exclusive treasure seems not to have been popularly sought.

5.
An Awful Heavy Suitcase
McGregor Gold
Clayton and Allamakee Counties

To the west, a more sought after treasure was planted by the same old man--a keg of money. It takes us back to the military road, mentioned earlier, about a quarter of the way to Fort Atkinson, where the Quarter Way House is perched on the edge of the Spanish Grant,[34] and near the present village of Girard [Giard]. A young farmer about 25 years old, living just north of Girard told the story.

"See that hedge row?" He pointed. "With the kind of a swale running along? That's the old military road. You used to could see the ruts. Runs straight as a die; the new road follows the ridge. Now see on the hillside yonder, where the road would run right past it if you could see it?"

He indicated now a jack-straw pile of brown timbers sprangling over a gray stone foundation.

"That's the old government barn. That's where the old man died and is buried, I guess. He's the one that brought the gold that's buried in our gold mine. He was coming on the military road, an carried an awful heavy suitcase, couldn't hardly drag it along. He coughed and he was scrawny and the fellow that kept the government barn--Pike, they say his name was--thought he acted queer but it wasn't none of his business.

"In the night this Pike saw the old man get up and go out but he thought it was just because he was sick. He was gone quite a spell, and when he came back he had the suitcase and he carried it easy. Soon after, the old man died. When morning come they found papers that let 'em know he'd had money.

IOWA LEGENDS OF BURIED TREASURE

Then they got word that a lot of money had been lost going to Fort Atkinson, about $50,000. So they knew the old man had buried the money somewhere kind of near and not very deep. "They dug for it, mostly up through those woods west. People say its buried in a keg. A keg was missing from the barn and people thought the old man used it.

"When I was a kid, a funny looking fellow named George Hawks came from Estherville. He had one of these gold finders. Looked kinda like a compass but it had gold on the point. He said it would point to gold. He wanted to look for the gold on shares, he said, and paw said it was all right and we kids went with him and helped him dig. We went down to the barn where the gold come from to pick up the scent. Sure 'nough, it pointed west to our timber. It took us across the road and down through the timber about three quarters of a mile to the hollow. There's a big sink hole there. The needle had been showing stronger and stronger signs all the way and when we got right up to the edge of that sink hole it showed awful strong signs.[35]

"We dug in the bottom of the hole. The dirt rolled down in from the edges, the sink hole sides are steep, and we had to carry a lot to the top. The gold needle kept on giving strong signs but when we got to solid rock we quit. Then my brother and I tried digging sideways, thinking maybe we had missed it, but that was more work still and we quit.

OLD DAN

Charlotte Kother Meyer of Girard [Giard] assures me that government agents once came to look for the treasure and that they dug holes but found no money. It was once the common practice among many of the neighbors to scuff their feet through suspicious places when in the vicinity of the old barn. One of the pioneers, Peter Farley, is said to have derived amusement from the legend. Daniel Bickel used to tell the story, and his nephew, Willie Bickel, a middle-aged civil engineer living in McGregor told it as it appears here.

An Awful Heavy Suitcase

"Uncle Dan, everybody called him, came here in the early day when he was a kid, sixteen, eighteen years old. He was a romantic young rascal. He and another fellow drove all day and half the night to see what two girls looked like--the first ones in the county. Uncle Dan used to tell this story and laugh. He worked for an old fellow named Peter Farley. Pete came down stairs one morning looking excited. 'I can find it', he says, 'Boys, I can find that gold.' Old Peter was the kind of man Uncle Dan called a 'stoten bottle.' Nobody ever found out just what that meant.

"There was another hired man there and he and Uncle Dan wanted to go dig it up then. 'No,' Pete told them. He said he'd dreamed just where the gold was, but he would have to go after it just the way the dream told him to.

"When the chores were done that night, Old Peter loaded them up with picks and shovels and grub hoes, but he didn't carry much himself. He was so busy remembering where to go he couldn't seem to carry anything.

"The boys didn't mind that, though. They couldn't wait. He took them out across a field and then he set down under a white oak tree. I always figured it was the one west of the old barn, and off by itself. He said they would have to wait till the shadow of a limb on this tree came to a certain spot at midnight.

"It was cold and Uncle Dan didn't have enough clothes on. Old Peter had a heavy coat. After they'd dug awhile, Old Peter decided there was only room for two and sat down under the tree. He'd done the dreaming and they could do the digging.

"They dug awhile and then hit a board. Then you should have seen the dirt fly. They just couldn't palpitate those shovels fast enough. It was a box all right and those two youngsters had the money about spent before they found it was a rough box with a baby's skeleton in it. Old Peter had remembered about an immigrant family burying a child there and had come out the night before to locate the right spot."

Such are the four versions of the loss of the Fort Crawford gold. Lieutenant Colonel L. S. Morey of the finance department in the War Department at Washington, has written[36] that his records show no abnormal sum of money

IOWA LEGENDS OF BURIED TREASURE

been sent for its completion and no recorded sum was lost. There is foundation, however, for a tale of buried treasure some thirty miles to the north: the New Albin Gold.

6.
Black Hawk
New Albin Gold
Allamakee County

The story depends upon a bit of local history, the massacre by which the Black Hawk uprising subsided. In 1832 in northwest Illinois, Black Hawk gained definite and unpopular victories. But, by the time the Indians had been crowded into Wisconsin, the contest had become glorious and very hard on them. They were overtaken at Bad Ax Bend and all ages and genders were butchered with no great nicety. While General Atkinson pushed from the rear, the steamboat "Warrior" came up from Prairie du Chien. The boat also gave Battle Island its name, sowing the scanty refuge with canister and corpses. A few prisoners were taken back to Prairie du Chien[37] but other warriors escaped.

Although the river is here approximately a mile from bank to bank, the stream is so dotted with islands that points are few at which a swim of greater than a half mile is required. The conflict came in August when the river was low and the water a comfortable temperature. Logs in the river supplied cover and buoyancy. Historians grant the probability of landings on the Iowa side[38] though there Black Hawk's people would face hostile Wabasha and Winnebagoes.

The legend comes from Mrs. Dora Timmerman of New Albin. A middle aged German widow, she was raised on a farm six miles west of town. In her quaint parlor, she spoke in a genial, rapid manner, with her slight accent.

IOWA LEGENDS OF BURIED TREASURE

"Well, I will tell you what I know about the gold and jewelries. One of the first t'ings I remember was Papa telling about it. We were standing in the yard, so, and a big light flash up, just like that. Papa said, 'Watch quick, where it is.'" We watched hard but right away, out it went, and then, Oh, My! How dark. Papa said, 'In the morning we see where the gold and jewelries are,' but in the morning we had kind of forgotten, I guess. We couldn't find any place at all. More times it did that. It was the gold will do that way when it lays in the ground a long time. I would go in the yard and t'ink, 'Maybe it fire, and this time I will find the gold.' Then it wouldn't give blazes at all. After while, when I wasn't ready at all, then it would blaze some and how could I see until it stopped? Then I didn't know where it was at all. That was what it did.[39]

"We used to hunt for it day times, too. Papa told us where. You know Black Hawk. He was killed just up to Victory. That was the money that was buried. Black Hawk's money. They had a big battle right across the river from here, the soldiers and Black Hawk. The soldiers won and they killed almost all the Indians. You know the Black Hawk tree? I've got a piece of it. I was down to Prairie visiting my sister-in-law and I broke a piece off. That's where Black Hawk hid after he jumped off the cliff, while his ankle that he broke was getting well, and then he got away. The soldiers killed almost all the other Indians, but one. He got on a horse and took all the gold they had, or jewels or what they got. He put it in a sack and carried it on the horse when he made the horse swim the river, you know how they can do. Well, they take a sack and tie it up, but they don't quite fill the sack, maybe half. Then they have half of that in one and half in the other end and they hang on the horse in front. Papa didn't know how much there was. How could anybody know? But the soldiers said the sack was as full as he could carry it that way.

"He swim across here and went out toward our farm. It wasn't our farm then, it would be all woods. The soldiers was after him. They thought it was Black Hawk because he had the gold. There was an open space sort of, and they saw him there. That's how we knew where to look for the gold. That's where the school house is now. Some more beyond that is a spring. It may be half mile. That's where they shot him. They saw him giving his horse a drink and they shot him and found him dead. But he had buried the gold and they couldn't find it.

Black Hawk

"We used to look for the gold, too. Papa showed us how. He said if you held the right kind of a willow stick over it, it would turn in your hands, so. Every time we went up to the spring for water--we would go at recess--we would all take sticks and walk with them in our hands. Lots of times I thought mine was going to turn, but it never did. I guess the right kind of willow didn't grow there. Papa used to tell us to use all kinds of sticks. 'Then you get the right one yet,' he would say. I guess we used about every kind that grew. Sometimes they would be a dozen, maybe, all carrying sticks. I scuffed my shoes or my bare feet at little pieces of dirt, every one I find. The old Indian buried the gold in a hole or just scraped the dirt and buried it shallow because pretty soon after the men saw him and he had the gold. They shot him. Then he didn't have the gold. I always thought how nice it would be if I could find that gold and jewelries but after while I came to town and then I didn't hunt any more."

This treasure trove seems to have grown less petulant and combustible with the years. In other respects it resembles another to the south, the story of the Andrew Treasure.

Black Hawk (MA-KA-TAI-ME-SHE-KIA-KIAH). Drawing from A. R. Fulton's book, *The Red Men of Iowa*.

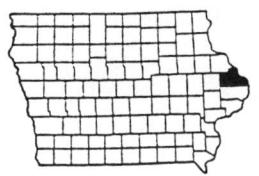

7.
A Kid, He Never Forgets
Andrew Gold
Jackson County

W. M. Herschelman told me this story, a farmer now above fifty-five years old. He lived on the edge of Andrew, a declining village that was once county seat of Jackson county. We talked in early evening. The milking was done and he leaned on the lower half of the barn door.

"There's one story might interest you, about some money, quite a bunch of it, buried down along the Indian trail that used to run between here and where the iron bridge is now, maybe along Brush Creek. I never dug for it myself, but I know many that did. I could give the the name of one of them. Lives in Maquoketa. He was diggin' right along side of the road in one of these Injun mows [mounds] as the saying is. O' course, I don't right know he was diggin' for that hunderd thousand dollars, but it just popped into my mind just as soon as I seed him. I'd been thinkin' 'bout the story--heard it when I was a kid and what a feller hears when he's a kid he never forgets-- and just when I seed this feller diggin' in that Indian mow it popped to me right away what he was diggin' for, but I didn't want to embarrass him by askin'. He wouldn't find it there, though. Not least the way I figure. I tell you why. The Siouxs was having a pow-wow down near where the iron bridge is now. Those other Indians that lived here and was moved west--who was they fightin'? Know it as well as I know my own name. Yes, that's right, Sacs and Foxes, yes. Well, they played traitor on the others, sold out to the whites and one Indian that had the money, he skipped and the Siouxs took after him and caught him and killed him along about in here

35

somewhere. But when they got him, he had buried the money already and it's there to this day. When the guv'ment moved the Indians there wasn't no trace of the money either.

"Now, the way I figure it, that Injun didn't have no time to go makin no mow. What he'd a-done would have been just hide that money some place he knew already in some cave or holler tree. I've always thought I'd take a week off some time when I didn't have nothing much to do and hunt through them caves or down along the creek. I'd done it before now, but I thought it'd be a week wasted, not knowin' just where to look, or nothin'. Course, you can't tell, I might be like that fella I heard about when I was a kid. And there was a funny thing, too. That didn't happen more'n four or five miles from here, down on the Green Island bottoms. A fellar was choppin' down a rotten tree and he found $28,000 in gold. Never knew how it come to be there, and maybe it wasn't so. I just heard it and a feller can't believe all he hears. Course, as far as that goes, I don't really know a thing more about this Injun money than you do; that was way before my time and all I know is what the old settlers told. I knowed the man that told me a good many years ago and he was reliable. The worst is, a feller doesn't know just where to look. I've thought maybe some time I'd investigate a lot of these big trees people has left standin' thinkin' they was hollow, but seems like I don't get around to it.

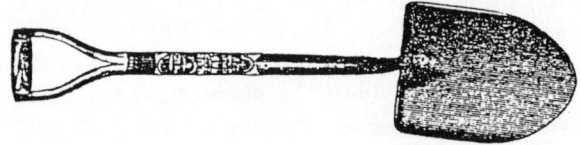

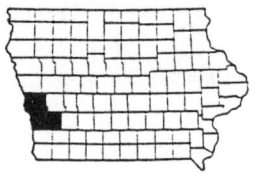

8.
Whiskey, Gold and Mules
Missouri River Money
Pottawattamie and Harrison Counties

A long time ago--maybe it was seventy years and maybe it was not--when the river transportation on the Missouri was still bustling, one of the greatest boats then plying the stream labored up along the Iowa shore. It labored with reason for its hold groaned, its gunwales bulged, its decks rose up in towers from the bulk of whiskey it carried. Even in those lush days it went its way moistly; with its engines breathing hard it trundled into the current like a fat lady in a pool.

Just what happened to that comfortable toper has not been recorded beyond dispute. Some will tell you that a boiler burst under the strain of breasting such a load against the current at a bend. Others will have it that the boat struck a snag and, being burdened almost to the swamping stage, went under without a groan.[40]

I first heard the story while following a remark of a Des Moines man, who "once heard tell that a whole bargeload of gold dust sank in the Missouri River, somewhere between Sioux City and Council Bluffs."

"Everybody in Council Bluffs," said Irving Grossman, a student at Drake University, "knows the story of that whiskey. The boat sank just south of town at a bend in the river. The river has shifted away from the bend until it became a backwater and eventually a lake. For a long time it was a resort and now the land is being made into a golf course. You see the boat tried to make land after the accident and sank just

IOWA LEGENDS OF BURIED TREASURE

away from the dock. With the shifting of the current the old river bottom, and hence the whiskey, is now in that gold course. Dry businessmen go out there, hot and thirsty, and every time they see an old board they think whiskey is near. Whenever anybody throws up a bunker they gather 'round in hope that the old pre-war will be uncovered."

"I've heard that story ever since I came here in 1876," Fire Chief Frank Hitchcock said. "I've had that spot pointed out to me a half dozen times, but it was always a different spot."

Jack DeWitt, star reporter and free lance writer on the *Council Bluffs Nonpariel*, vouches for the story. "There isn't anything to that gold dust yarn,[41] but the whiskey. She was a freighter plying between St. Louis and Sioux City and the shipment of whiskey can be traced from Chicago to St. Louis, and then on up the river. A fellow named Smith captained her. Named 'Mary Lou', she had $6,000 worth of whiskey aboard. There were 2,000 kegs and 1,000 gallons bottled.

"She wasn't sunk down at Lake Manawa, though. They're all wrong about that. She lays up about thirty miles[42] north of here, and the shifting of the river has left her out in a farmer's corn field. He's got the wheel house and uses it for a chicken coop. There she is, and you ought to be able to spot her with a little intelligent looking around."

Mrs. Hattie Harl, a secretary and historian, remembered a boat that was sunk with its treasure, but it, too, was a boat going up the river, rather than a barge of dust coming down from the mountains.

"I remember that a boat was coming from St. Louis with a payroll for some fort up the river," she told me. "Something happened to it, it struck a snag or it blew up and though most of the people were saved, a lot of money went down with it.

Warren Huff, former bank president, now about eighty-five years old, thought this boat might be the same he had heard of, a government boat that anchored about the same place. It bore mules for Fort Pierre and went under when "a great big tree fell plump onto them and sank them straight and drowned all the mules."

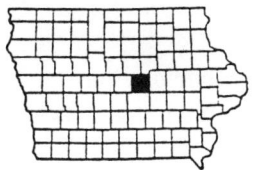

9.
North Skunk Kettle
State Center Gold
Marshall County

John White, debate coach at Council Bluff's high school, started me on the trail of another transported treasure: the State Center Gold.

Land to the northwest of Newton rolls heavily, contains marshy valleys and many rounded hills that nurtured timber and citizens. Through this territory, at the time of the Civil War, a stagecoach route lazed up toward Edenville on a regular basis.

"I remember," said White, "the old timers telling of a pot of gold buried at the foot of an oak tree. Indians beset an old man on the trail about eight miles north of what is now State Center. He was known to carry gold, but none was found after the attack. How they knew about where to dig, I don't know. But they dug and dug. There was supposed to be a pot about the size of a peck measure and should have measured around $10,000."

Later John White wrote me: "My father tells me the following. During the Civil War the stagecoach running between Newton, Iowa, and Edenville, Iowa, was attacked by robbers along the branch of the North Skunk River about one mile east and eight miles south of State Center, Iowa.

"A United States mail sack containing considerable money was hastily buried by one of the members of the stagecoach party who anticipated the attack. This member was soon called to war and never returned. Consequently the exact location of the buried treasure was never discovered and the money was never recovered.

"My father came here (about one and a half miles north of the approximate place of the buried gold) in 1876. However, I

IOWA LEGENDS OF BURIED TREASURE

believe that a certain Charles Flora of Rhodes [initially called Edenville], Iowa, was living there at that time and now owns the land upon which the treasure is buried.

"All the facts about the stagecoach are beyond dispute, but whether or not that gold was buried, of course, is unknown. However, it is common opinion that the Flora boys spent many days digging for the treasure but never found it."

The elder Mr. White later added that the mail sack was thought to have been put in a kettle, and from Charles Flora I had the following version: "A man had stolen some money somewhere, it was down south I believe. He was afraid he was goin' to get caught, so when he got along about here he buried it. He'd been robbin' a bank or something, I heard. He was comin' up through here on the stagecoach. They was $40,000 of it and (it was buried) in the first grove north of the North Skunk that joins the South Skunk just a little south of here. That'd make it right down here in our pasture. They's some thought it was the second grove. One of the trees was grubbed out afore we come here."

Floyd Roberts, a young farmer to the east, also owns the land on which this treasure lies.

"Yes, I guess there's money buried here all right; 'least that's what they all say." He talked on the subject very readily. "I've never dug for it myself, but when I was a little feller, a bunch of the farmers dug up the whole yard looking for it. They was waiting for Pa to go thrashing with 'em and as a bunch of men will, you know, they got to joshin' about that treasure. One of 'em asked Pa if he cared if they dug for the treasure. Of course he said, 'No,' and they didn't do a thing for the next half hour but just make a garden out of the whole backyard and most of the barnyard. You may be just about standing on that gold right now.

"When my grandfather was a young man and owned this farm--Grandpa'd be a little over a hundred now if he was alive. They was an old man lived here in a log cabin when Grandpa got the land and Grandpa just let him stay. This was all timber country, heavy timber country, in them days. I can remember it so you couldn't hardly go through it in the grove out there where that barn stands now.

"Well, this old man he got awful sick after that and he had somebody fetch his brother. He told the brother that he had

North Skunk Kettle

robbed the bank of $50,000 and brought it out here on the stagecoach, put it in one of them big iron kettles, put a box over it. He said he couldn't die peaceable until the gold was found. The brother went out and looked between the two hickory trees like the old man told him, but he didn't find nothing. The old man got worse and every little while he would send the brother out to look. Finally he died.

"When Grandpa wanted to come here to live the brother didn't like to go away and leave that gold. He told Grandpa about it and they agreed to go halves, but they never found it. Pa wrote to one of the companies that advertized treasure-finding machines in the farm paper once, but they said they didn't send out their machines on shares, and Pa didn't get one. He said if the money was there we'd prob'ly find it anyway some time.

"If it was ever there, it's there yet and I don't see why it wouldn't be. The hickory trees are cut now, but they were still standing when I was a boy. One stood there back of that gate in the yard and the other cut toward the barn like. That'd make the kettle 'bout where you're standin' maybe, and I remember she was buried about two and a half feet down."[43]

There are other available locations for the treasure. My informants agree that it was buried in the first, second or third grove on the Skunk, but on which Skunk? Further, trees grew in wallpaper patterns, and even where they were bunched, how many trees are required for a grove? How many were required in 1864?

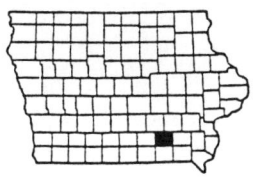

10.
After My Death
Eddyville Treasure
Wapello County

Eddyville rests in that peace not common outside vacation folders. All small towns in the Middle West have their somnolent aspects, but old towns, small for many years, attain a calm like the flavor of fruit which appears only at ripening. That Eddyville was to be a small town became certain when the railroad went its commercial way through Ottumwa. And a fever for real estate, which the rumor of rails had engendered, left many an enthusiast lot-poor.

This same fever, however, provided one of Eddyville's few diversions. Perhaps the fever's only rival rose out of a sealed box that arrived for W. W. DeLong, editor of *The Tribune* and postmaster of Eddyville. Elaborately sealed in red wax, it commanded attention like the lifted hand of a priest. Large letters on the outside said, TO BE SENT UNOPENED TO THE POSTMASTER AT EDDYVILLE AFTER MY DEATH.[44]

A companion letter, written in an unpracticed hand on tablet paper read:
"Mr. Postmaster
"Eddyville, Ia.:
"Three days ago there died at my house in this city, Mr. Jerome LeBarge, a man with a checkered and turbulent career. He came to my house four months ago in very feeble health. He seems to have no relatives or friends, but he always paid his board regularly. Something seemed to always prey

upon his mind. What it was he never told, but he would frequently start up from a sound sleep, the cold sweat breaking from every pore, seemingly trying to escape some awful influence that was stifling him.

"He died in a perfect frenzy of convulsions, begging for mercy and screaming with terror of some unseen thing. It was horrible.

"His secret died with him unless this packet, which he made me promise to send unopened to the postmaster at Eddyville, Iowa, contains the key.

"In fulfillment of his last request, I ask you to see to it that his dying wishes, if not unreasonable, be respected.

Very truly,
Mrs. Jos. Snow
Pittsburg, Pa."

If this letter intrigued the postmaster, the contents of the sealed package must have transported him. It contained a lengthy document and a map showing signs of age, but flaring with red ink. Both purported to be the work of the convulsioned LeBarge. The former told how Jerome LeBarge followed the whispers of hidden gold and had done well if not handsomely in the early part of the Badlands gold rush of 1878. By dint of hard work he made a comfortable living and when he found two likely miners with nothing but empty pockets and headaches, "grubstaked" them. The ledge they uncovered was sold for $45,000 and the three started back, in company and in bad temper. They drank to accord with their new status and while they were sober enough, spent the evenings playing cards. At this last, a big fellow who called himself William Gunton had all the luck that was good and his pal, one Melalley, evened the scale out of his gold pouch and his conviviality. By the time the party had crossed South Dakota and worked as far down into Iowa as Eddyville there was very little good humor left among them, and Gunton had most of the gold. In reviewing the document for his readers DeLong quoted a considerable part of the confession:[45]

"The crisis came one night while we were camping about a mile northeast of a little town called Eddyville, Iowa. Our camp was pitched in a lonesome place, under a couple of small oaks in the turn of the road. The nearest house was half a mile

After My Death

east, while on the road south were two graveyards. There were few passers.

"As usual we were all pretty drunk and we started the inevitable game of cards. Melalley had been morose and sullen all day and was very quarrelsome. Bill was having his usual run of good luck, while Malalley threw his money belt containing all that was left of his $15,000 on the ground in front of him, staking it all on his hand. When he called he threw down four kings; Bill had a straight. Melalley accused Bill of cheating. With an oath Bill made a drunken lunge at Melalley with his hunting knife, laying open his arm. Melalley grabbed up a wagon stake and hit Bill a terrific clout just back of the left ear. He felt like an ox. I sprang to stop them, but Bill didn't budge. A hurried examination revealed his skull was crushed. He gasped several times and was dead.

"The horror of the crime sobered us. Gunton now had all of Melalley's money and most of mine. We knew Gunton to be an assumed name. He never spoke of any relatives. To escape the consequences of our deed, did it become known, would be difficult. There was but one thing to do and that was to hide all traces of the crime, divide the money and put all possible distance between us and this spot.

"Hurriedly dragging the body back from the firelight, with a knife we ripped off his clothing, rifling his pockets of everything that might afford a clue to his identity. I threw his garments into the campfire, and just as I finished Melalley stepped up holding in his hand a grewsome object. It was Gunton's head, bloody and dripping, severed from the trunk. Holding it up by the long reddish hair, the bloated countenance, the protruding eyeballs, the sneering lips still seemingly cursing--a horrible sight--he tossed it into the fire. Writhing and twisting, the flames gnawed and scorched off flesh and hair, destroying the surest means of identification.

"A dark woods bordered the road on the west and into it, across a small ravine, we carried the headless trunk. Hurriedly digging a four-foot hole, we jammed the body in, trampling the ground down and carefully removing all evidence of its disturbance.

"Going back to the fire, the nauseating stench of the burning flesh warned us that the head would be long in burning. So, stepping out into the road, I buried the head in the middle of the wagon track, depending on the passing travel to obscure all traces of its hiding place.

"We then scattered our campfire over the place where the butchery had taken place, to cover all traces of blood, hitched up our team and hurriedly left the scene. By daybreak we were twenty miles from the spot, and though years have passed the crime was never discovered."

A summary of the remainder of the letter was added by DeLong who apparently did not doubt that the two were haunted by the sights and deeds of that night. Melalley is said to have died the following year in a hospital, raving in delirium and torn by paroxysms while he cried and screamed and occasionally begged a dripping head to have mercy upon him. LeBarge, by his professed confession, a nervous wreck, still fled the gory one down the labyrinthine ways of many boarding houses, and, also by his professed confession, never cared nor dared return to the spot of the murder, although he was sure his soul would be tortured as his body had been until the wronged felt the cool of sacred earth.

So much the editor printed and promised that another week would bring forth a map of the murder, which "we intended to present to our readers in this issue, but owing to the sickness of the editor the greater part of the week, prevented him from engraving it in time for this issue."

The next issue of *The Tribune* carried little but a reprint of what was credited to *The Des Moines Daily News* of November 11. The quoted passages told that "hundreds are digging like beavers today in Eddyville in the vain hope that they may stumble upon the body while W. W. DeLong secretly watches for the discovery of the treasure."[46]

News of this treasure, it seems, had been unearthed through the adroitness of one of *The News* sleuths, who provided the information that $30,000 had been buried near the skeleton and charged that "part of the story detailing wealth to the finder and enabling him to find it by means of a map, was carefully withheld from the public."[47] That DeLong was concerned with carrying out even this last injunction of the letter, is doubtless understandable, but that he was thoroughly sincere in the whole matter is probably indicated by his printing along with this clipping, information that he declared had come to him in answer to letters addressed to the Pittsburg board of health. He

After My Death

quoted this official (missing?) that no Jerome LeBarge had of late died in Pittsburg and that no Mrs. Joseph Snow was there or had been recently operating a boarding house there.

"Most everybody 'round here was up there next Sunday," Sid Crosson confided to me. "They got tired of it, though. You heard about us findin' that old bone? C____ B____ was night marshall awhile back--that was when I was day marshall--had done quite a bit of diggin' and when he went down into Arkansas he consulted one of these here clairvoyants. Seems like she knew about him huntin' treasure, least that's what he said, and she told him about it and she says, 'You want to go on beyond, on beyond,' she says, 'and then you'll find a tree and at the foot of the tree you'll find an old bone.' And that's where he was to dig.

"C____ come back pretty excited and he says to me, 'You got that map and them letters?'

"I did have, then. DeLong had give 'em to me to keep when he went east to Indianny. We didn't do nothin' durin' the week, but Sunday afternoon I didn't have nothin' to do and C____ come around so I says, 'Spose we go up there, just for fun.' He was 'greeable and I got the map and that treasure probe[48] there and we went up. I'd made that rod right on that forge when they had the first diggin'; it's come awful handy locating water mains and the like.

"Well, we went up there. You know how the land lays? Well, the road comes around a hill, new moon like, on the far side of the graveyard. On the turn there is a black oak tree and beyond it is a gulch. 'Tother side of that gulch is another black oak tree. You sight from the center of the road to where the head is buried, to those two trees and then you pace fifty paces down that line and where you find the body, you make a square on it ten paces each way and the other three corners has $10,000 apiece. We got the line all right and then we got to know that holler well.

"Right up atop the hill, kind of by itself like, was another black oak tree smack in line. Underneath that tree, right where the clairvoyant said it'd be, we found one of them mastodon teeth. I give it to DeLong cause he's got arrow heads.

"C____ got purty excited and he thought we was goin' to find that gold right then. We poked around some with the probe, but we didn't strike nothin'. We didn't dig any; the folks up there don't like it much.

"I wa'n't never much of a hand to believe in them clairvoyants, but I'd like to know how she knowed that bone was there. I always figured one of her relatives put it there."

In the fall of 1920[49] road graders turned out a skull some ten feet from where Bill's grisly head was said to have lain. Editor DeLong then told the confession of John Steel, who died in prison for killing a neighbor in a fenceline brawl and who with two others, "Uncle Bobbie" Oldham and James Wylie, had dug the head from the old roadbed years before.

"Then they went to digging all over again," Mr. DeLong said. "There was one bunch of dynamiters came here and wanted me to make 'em a map. The original, you know, was stolen from Sid Crosson, along with other papers. Personally, I am now inclined to believe there is no money there, that the head was that of a man who left here with a young actor. From the dramatic style of those letters, I always thought they were written by the actor, who had murdered his companion for his money and used this trick to get the body a decent burial. Some years ago I was out to the hollow where the gold is supposed to lie and saw several ridges, as though some one had been digging long holes. The skeleton, I think, has long ago been removed, but there was a time when I believed as much as anyone in the treasure."

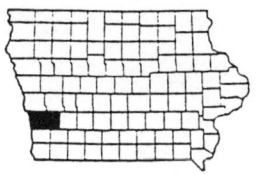

11.
Jack the Fire King
1920 Council Bluffs Mail Robbery
Pottawattamie County

While this robbery[50] is too new for legend, it is the stuff from which legends are made. Keith Collins and Fred Poffenbarger are said to have confessed to removing $3,500,000 from nine mail sacks. That they could neither divert suspicion nor remove the negotiables far proved their undoing. Little of the treasure had been spent before they went to Leavenworth, Kansas.

When the money hunt began, coin was found by the barrel with the chinks between the dollars melted full and the package appropriately marked, LARD. Dresser drawers were full of negotiables. Through the confession of "Jack the Fire King" in Des Moines, $5,000 in bonds were found "buried twelve feet from a big tree."[51] It was the scene of a gun battle on Lena Schneider's farm near town. There, hidden under burlap beneath a chicken coop, were $10,000 worth of traveler's checks taken from the Drake Park bank in Des Moines. When the wild scramble had about worn itself out, there was still over $500,000 missing, some in bullion, but mostly bonds.[52]

The largest visible shortage was that of $438,000 in bonds and $2,000 in cash that the two prisoners declared was thrown from the Douglas Street Bridge between Omaha, Nebraska, and Council Bluffs. On the run, they secreted all but one satchel full of bonds and a little cash. Into this, according to Collins' testimony, two cobblestones were dropped in and the whole pitched out of a taxi crossing the Missouri River. The reason for this act was not entirely explained to Judge Martin

J. Wade, but there would have been less suspicion had not Collins made an unguarded remark.

"It's all right", Collins said before his trial. "We'll do our time and then we'll be rich when we get out. I've got lots of those bonds planted."[53]

Some people suggested Collins' cronies might live modestly for a few years and then melt away to other climes and live like plutocrats if there wasn't more treasure hunting. To stimulate this point of view came the information early in 1925 that coupons from the missing bonds were trickling into the home offices.[54]

The transportation motive in the stories, the eccentricities of characters, the violence and burials, and the possibility that a fortune waits out there for the hunter--from such comes legend.

Part 2
GOLD THAT FLED VIOLENCE

Gold in its consorting with unconventional people came sooner or later to bed, to the grave and to an immortality through its legends of buried treasure.

Many buryings grow out of the natural life of the border. Unrighteous blood has ever been mixed with gold, and if there have been in Iowa no one-leg, one-eye, one-cut pirates; no gang planks for innocents and no coral reefs for their wealth, there have nevertheless been men, violently dead. Bandits, finding sudden wealth incriminating and bunglesome, buried it.

But, money not buried by rascals is as like to have been cashed by the righteous. Tin cans beneath hedges, bottles under great trees, wallets crammed down cracks in the chicken house floor and homespun stockings under the mattress constituted the reserve bank of the time.

Deposits in the ground often proved safe even from those who would withdraw their holdings. Mortality among depositors was a thing of terror.

Thus, pioneer money, whether it passed through the hands of the righteous or the riotous came eventually to those great vaults of the International Bank of Banditry. From thence the legends grew.

IOWA LEGENDS OF BURIED TREASURE

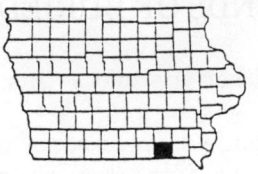

12.
Bushwackers
Bloomfield Treasure
Davis County

Gordon Westby, a retired farmer living in Marengo, told me the story.

"Old John Wallace used to live on what they called the Gore place, and I reckon they call it that yet. Old John hadn't much of a fambly--just the woman and Willie. He was a right hard worker and he laid by quite a bit. It was war times, prices was good. John was too old to go and Willie was too young and they didn't have a danged thing to do but make money, and they did it.

"Them was bushwhackin' days. Old John lived just this side of the Missouri line. We did too. They had a war down there once, or would of if the Iowans had been ready to fight when the Missourians was ready. When the Iowans got there the Missourians had gone. We didn't like the fellers in Missouri and they didn't waste no lovin' on our side. But when the War of the Rebellion come along, they liked our mules well enough and they come over at night and took 'm. I spose some of our boys sniped their cows.

"Old John had laid by three thousand in gold and got to worryin' the Missourians would get it. They'd shot Captain Bence and some of his militia and Old John took he money outa the Troy bank.

"'What'll I do if you git killed?' his wife says. 'Ain't I got a right to some of that money anyhow? How'm I goin' to raise the kid?'

"He thought the only way to keep a woman still was not to tell her nothin' but it wa'n't long b'fore he changed his mind some 'bout that. He give her seven hundred-fifty and he buried the rest. Neither one told t'other where they'd buried their share.

"One day some mule buyers come along and Old John suspicioned 'em. They didn't buy no mules and Old John reckoned they wanted to steal his mules that night or dig his money. A neighbor come over, name of Duffield or Huffman, and they sent a man to town to git the militia. A widder woman come over and said the mule fellers had been gettin' fresh and were in her shack.

"Old John and his boy and Duffield 'cided they'd ketch them mule buyers, not likin' to have 'em around there that night. When they got guns and knocked on the widder's door the mule fellers came out as nice as you please. Sure they'd come and why all the guns, and such. But they wanted to git their coats. What they got was their guns and they come back out that door a spittin' fire. All the farmers was shot and Old John died. The boy got four or five bullets, but he was a tough 'un.

"The mule fellers went to a neighbor and told how Old John had been murdered and asked the way to town so they could raise a posse. The neighbor rushed off to town and the mule fellers stole his horses and used 'em to get out of the county.

"The old woman died purty soon after and they ain't nobody ever found that money so fur as I know, though they was a lot hunted for it. Yes, I've looked 'round a bit myself in what I thought was likely places, but not the way some of 'em did."[55]

William (Judge) Fox of Bellevue and points both south and west is thought to have buried money at many points along the Mississippi River.

"There is an historical reference to his treasure at the mouth of the Des Moines River. After killing and robbing Colonel George Davenport [July 4, 1845], Fox and his men escaped south by dint of stolen skiffs, a good current and emancipated plow horses. When the party reached the Iowa border, Fox convinced a woman that he was a tailor, purchased beeswax, and after melting it on a hot stone, sealed their loot into empty bottles. John Long is said to have made the following confession: "At a point where Fox left Birch to go and bury the money, he made the figures 72 on a large black walnut tree. Seventy-two yards from this tree in a northeastern direction is a small black walnut tree with a

Bushwackers

bowie knife; fourteen yards from this small tree, due north, is a large stone; midway between the tree and the stone is the spot where the money was buried."[56]

Fox figures also in another Bellevue treasure.

IOWA LEGENDS OF BURIED TREASURE

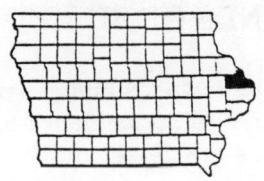

13.
The Bellevue War
Bellevue Treasure
Jackson County

Whether or not marauders actually founded Bellevue, versatile bandits early showed no aversion to it.[57] Chief among them was a certain Brown who operated one of the famous early hostelries of the state. He was a villain to pattern by. His face was long and pronged with appropriate curving black whiskers; his body was as spare and powerful as his saturnine face required, and his skin was either of a villainous pallor or of a dark threatening hue, as you wish. "To steal horses, to pass counterfeit money and dispense justice did not seem incongruous to this many-minded man of evil deeds."[58] In spite of his foreboding front he was noted for his professional hospitality. There seems also to have been a Robin Hood legend about him, that he gave much of what he stole to the poor. General belief made him leader of the so-called "Banditti of the Prairies," and his jovial hotel [Bellevue House] the center of roguery for all that rascal-infested region. "The Big Woods" to the west had their unfortunate connotations in matters equestrian: the wild lands and caverns north of Maquoketa were not without suspicion nor errant nags: "Horse Thief Cave" north of Anamosa did not get its name by accident.[59]

Thus, in popular belief, Brown was a proper villain. Not only did he conduct political matters boldly, manage rascals genially and absorb obligingly, but he was thought to entertain ambitions

IOWA LEGENDS OF BURIED TREASURE

with both the virtuous and generous ladies. When a hired girl arrived at the dance hall, her wits and her night clothes scattered and her body covered with blood, one of Brown's men was shot on the street. Fox is said to have retaliated with a gun powder plot that was almost a success.

Such is the legendary or historical setting of the Bellevue War. Louis Efferding, eighty years old, an axe handle maker and a native, reported the popular version of the fight and its subsequent treasure:

"What I know about the Bellevue War [1840] was telled me by them as was there. We had a neighbor, name of Smith, was down to it and they was more. You see, W. W. Brown was the backbone of it. He had his place, a hotel I guess you'd call it, full of men he had workin' for him. They'd steal horses in Illinois, run 'em across on the ferry and Fox or some of 'em would jump on 'em and ride west. They'd sell 'em one to the other and if they got caught they'd swear the horse was sold to the man that had it. One of our neighbors, Graham his name was, lost a horse and they catched the feller as did it and the whole Brown gang sweared he bought the horse. Graham couldn't do nuthin'. Brown was justice of the peace. Finally the people that had been stole from worked it up quiet and sixty of 'em gathered under the river bluff. It was done quiet, but Brown must've got wind of it. He had sixty or seventy men in his hotel, or maybe he was always ready. The farmers sent a man up with a white flag to offer to let him surrender, but Brown stood right in the doorway and wouldn't do it.

"The boys upstairs'll s'render in a minute," he says, and with that their guns started crackin' and of course the farmers shot back. Brown was shot twict I know and maybe three times. They was a lot of shootin' and some was killed on either side and finally the farmers won. They held a vote. Some say it was with beans. White beans for hangin' and colored beans for lickin' and sendin' down the river. The white beans won by one vote and Fox and the others was put on a raft and sent down the river. They told 'em they'd kill 'em if they ever come back.

"Fox did, though, come back in about a week. I think it was at night. There weren't no railroads then and you had to travel at night as well as day. You see, they hadn't found

The Bellevue War

Brown's money. Folks thought he must have been pretty well fixed. He had them men workin' for him and he wouldn't have hardly done it for nothin'. Maybe Fox knew where Brown kept his money, or maybe he had some of his own. He wasn't much of but a common horse thief himself. Still, I guess, no matter how bad a man he was, some friends had prob'ly they warned him he better not stay, because he got out before the farmers could do nothin'. About thirty of 'em rode in to town after him. He must've come back after money; I can't figure any other reason why he should. Some thought it was buried in what they called the City Well, right over on that corner. They find rock there yet, plowin', but that was before my time."

An opposite point of view was expressed by the Hon. James Ellis, of Maquoketa, a collector and the author of the Jackson county history. He is now about seventy-five years old.
"Brown, W. W. Brown, who was either the hero or the martyr of the Bellevue War, may have buried money. There was a belief that he did and after his death a party of rowdies dragged Mrs. Brown to the river and threatened to set her adrift on a plank if she would not tell where it was hidden, but I am not sure that there was more to his estate than what was evident. He had a great deal of real property and much of that was swindled from him by the Confederates.

"He was a Yankee, a good businessman, and many old settlers told me he was the best man in the county. He came here to build up the country. He hired men to cut wood and he sold it to the steamboats. He was making money and the Confederates didn't like it. The whole war was nothing but a feud between Yankees and the Confederates. The southerners--they came from Kentucky; Brown was a New England man--had the semblance of the law with Captain Warren, who'd got to be sheriff some how and Colonel Cox was on their side. Cox had been congressman and s'posed he would be nominated at the Democratic caucus again, but Brown got it by one vote. Cox was a powerful man and a hard drinker. He cared nothing for other people and was used to having his way. He and his men signed a sworn statement that they would drive Brown out of town or kill him.

"But that wasn't easy. You see, Brown hired a lot of men and he wasn't afraid of anybody. They would stick by him and some horse runners and other questionable people stayed with him. Cox accused Brown of harboring cutthroats and horse thieves, but the farmers knew Brown was all right and the Confederates had to bring men over from the Galena mines when they wanted trouble. They chose a time when a couple of steamers was docked. They got the deckhands drunk, handing out free whiskey by the tin cupful and with about sixty men attacked the hotel.

"Brown stood in the doorway and covered Colonel Cox with a rifle and Mrs. Brown was right behind to hand him guns. Captain Warren called out that if he would s'rrender, he and his men would not be hurt. Brown thought Warren was his friend, discharged his gun into the ground and allowed two of Cox's men to get to a window behind him. They shot him, one through the neck and one through the temple and some say a third man shot him too.

"There was a fight after that, the ten or twelve Yankees holding out against the sixty Confederates. Fox and some more was wounded trying to get out the back way. They were tried, licked and sent down the river. The Confederates weren't satisfied and tried to find Brown's money. They thought he had considerable because he did lots of business, but I don't know that they found any. They took Mrs. Brown down to the river. She was a wonderful woman, refined, quiet and loyal. They threatened to send her down the river on a plank unless she told where the money was hid, but if she knew at all they couldn't make her tell."

Mrs. Anna Wilson, a daughter of one of the first families and now eighty-nine years old, told me the following: "The money in the well? Have you heard about that? I know about that money. I'm one of the few that does know and what I didn't get from Mrs. Schaub herself I did get from Adelaide Smithers. Adelaide and I was girl chums before she was a Smithers. That house she lived in there was the one the rebels were in when the citizens attacked them. She took me up there one day and they was holes in the walls where the bullets came through and one corner of the room was black all over from the blood. 'Ain't you never washed up that blood?' I says to her and she says, 'We've washed and we've scrubbed, but it don't never get no differunt than you see.' She thought maybe it was because the blood was scalded in when it was first washed, but

The Bellevue War

anyway it didn't come off. Adelaide and I was chums and she used to let me use her schoolbooks and when she was married to Smithers and moved to Calliforny the Schaubs came there and one day Mrs. Schaub she told me some more.

"A feller came there, trampy looking he was, and said he was cleaning wells. He said that was his business to go around cleaning wells, and he would like to clean her well. Now, her well was the City Well when we had what they called the Bellevue War. She said the well was all right and she didn't want to pay money for having it cleaned. He told her what a bit of good he would do the well and how cheap, but she said, 'No.' Then he said he would clean the well for nothing. That made her 'spicious and she said she didn't want him around her well, that he could get out. She knew he wouldn't clean no well for nothing if they wasn't something else afoot. He argied and he argied, but she wouldn't let him clean it and finally he went off like she told him. Then she got to thinking and she knew right off that he was looking for money in that well and she told me she bet it was Old Fox come back after the money of his they never found. She said she wished then she had found out his name and noticed what he looked like. And she told me this her very self."

IOWA LEGENDS OF BURIED TREASURE

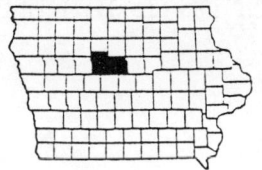

14.
Boone River Mound
Boone Gold
Webster and Hamilton Counties

The following is a letter that came to me too late to be investigated. It is included here, touching as it does the two groups of legends following.

"Stratford, Iowa
"June 4, 1927

"Wallaces' Farmer:
"Dear Sir:
"Am sending a sketch of history pertaining to the buried treasure in request of the article I read in the Wallaces' Farmer.
"Years ago, dating back as far as 1849, horse thieves, who then were quite plentiful, hid their loot in an Indian mound, at the mouth of the Boone River, as told by the old settlers.
"This mound is covered with a thick cluster of trees and is said to be hiding very valuable treasures.
"This mound is also near the Lott monument who was the first white man to settle here, and who with his family, was massacred by the Indians.
"This mound can be found on the farm of Y. Landreth who is a survivor of the 1850's. This treasure has been dug for but not found.

(Signed) "Miss Ruby Akins
"C/O Y. Landreth"

The John [Henry] Lott[60] mentioned here is well known in Iowa history and still more prominent in Iowa legend. He probably touched off the Spirit Lake massacre.

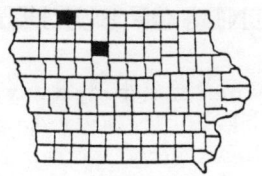

15.
Six Hogsheads
Livermore Whiskey
Humboldt and Dickinson Counties

[Henry] Lott was certainly an ingenious trader and probably a versatile scoundrel. He incurred the enmity of Sidominadotah, the chief of the Two Fingers tribe, a branch of the Sioux, and was forced to leave Boone. When Sidominadotah came north, where Lott had again prospered with beads and barrels, the white man disguised himself and his step-son as Indians. They visited the chief's lodge, and in a series of ambushes butchered all of the family except a ten year old girl and one Indian boy who had been left for dead.[61] The recovery and the information he brought was enough to send Lott down the Des Moines River fleeing the wrath of Inkpadutah. Lott left his wife to receive as much of punishment as one woman could bear. Inkpadutah was the brother of Sidominadotah, and he it was who massacred people north of Boone and again at Spirit Lake. Wherever he went, treasure seems to have descended before him.

Jack Barnes of Des Moines, a student, once worked in Humboldt County. "Would a lot of old whiskey be a buried treasure?" he asked. "Well, I know where there is six hogshead full of it. There was money, too, but it was the whiskey everybody was digging for.

"It's on the William Cox farm, about a mile and a half east of Livermore, in Humboldt County. When I was there, they used to play baseball every Sunday. Right near the baseball diamond it was quite a sport to dig that whiskey. We'd play until we got hot and then somebody'd say, 'Let's go out and dig up that Johnson whiskey.' It was quite a sport around there. Some of the older fellows would go over in the grove and poke around 'til they got cooled off.

"Either the Indians was going to the Spirit Lake massacre or coming from it, and I think they were going up there. A trader named Locke [Lott] killed an Indian chief. That made 'em mad and people were afraid of a massacre. Locke had been a trader, and there were three brothers whose name was Johnson who were traders also. They had six hogsheads of whiskey that they were going to use trading with the Indians, but when they heard of the trouble they were afraid the Indians would come and drink it up for nothing and go on the warpath sure. They rolled all these hogsheads out back of their log cabin and buried them in the woods.

"The woods were thick then, and the house stood right where the barn stands now. That didn't save 'em though. The Indians came along and killed all three of 'em and nobody was ever able to find that whiskey. They say there's gold buried all along Bloody Run, too. Not very much in a place but all the settlers had a little and they buried different places along the river. Some of 'em were killed and most of the rest of 'em didn't find much of theirs because that river is always shifting here and there and overflowing."

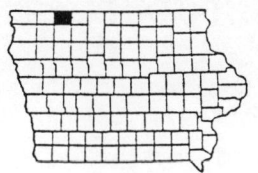

16.
Marble's Gold
Spirit Lake Treasure
Dickinson County

When Inkpadutah went farther north, more gold precipitated before him. The following is from a letter written by Mrs. Minnie Kingman Bergman of Spirit Lake and available through *The Des Moines Register:*

". . . 'I was born in Spirit Lake in 1861 and in my childhood heard so much about Indians, and my family had gone through so much, that was all we could talk about. The Marble family that were all killed had one daughter who was taken captive by the Indians. They lived on the west shore of Spirit Lake on the farm that is now the Birl Maish farm. When Mr. Marble found the Indians were coming, he had fifteen hundred dollars in gold that they buried some place on that farm. It has never been found. The pioneers used to hunt for it, I remember. The Marble girl was taken captive the same time Abbie Gardner-Sharp was taken. R. A. Smith in the history of Dickinson County speaks of it. Now this is just an outline of a buried treasure. My home is still in Spirit Lake, about two miles from the Marble Place. . . ."[62]

IOWA LEGENDS OF BURIED TREASURE

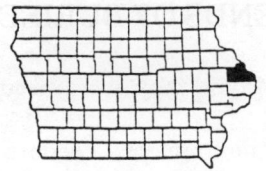

17.
Pest House
Bellevue Bandit Gold
Jackson County

Miss Akins indicated, horse thieves were given credit for burying money. Some of it was in the Bellevue Bandit Gold.

One of my informants was Mrs. Anna Wilson of Bellevue.

"There may be some buried treasure up at the old pest house," she hazarded. "Nobody knows, I guess. It's a stone house and it stands out southwest of town yet, I guess. It was built when I was a little girl by some horse thieves. They were driven out of there, or people thought they were, but there were queer noises after and some one was shot there when they were driven out. Some said the noises were made by wildcats in the cellar. Others said the noises were made by ghosts.

"Anyway," Mrs. Wilson went on, "nobody seemed to want to live there and the place stood vacant after the McDonnells moved out.

"Up back of the house a ways is a cave and below this cave there was a farmer plowing when the earth caved in with him. He had an awful time getting his horses out. They had fallen into an underground room and were struggling in their harnesses. When he did get them out, he wondered if that could have been the hiding place of the horse thieves or counterfeiters. He found kettles and cooking things in there.

"After while people named Halfhill came to visit. They were told about the haunted house. They were shown the cave and went back in farther, where nobody had gone before and they found four skeletons lying there like they had died and not been buried. Maybe they were brought there when they died.

"Then a man by the name of Theodore Winekopf bought the haunted house. One day his daughter, digging in the cellar struck a big ring. The man in the bank said it was a counterfeiter's ring. The money that's buried there may be counterfeit. I don't know.

"The house has been the pest house quite a while now."

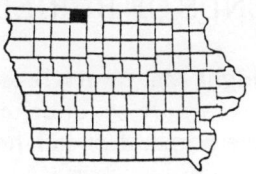

18.
Island Cellar
Gruver Gold
Emmet County

This legend comes from Wilbur Brood, through the *Wallaces' Farmer.*

"The time of the story," wrote Wilbur Brood, "dates back to the time of my grandfather in the year 1895.

"A band of horse thieves moving southwestward across the United States, passing through the northwest part of Iowa, suddenly came upon a large lake which was an out-of-the-way place and seldom visited. In the center of the lake an island was discovered which was grown over with trees and brush. As this was an excellent place for the thieves to carry out their plans and thefts from surrounding settlers and horse and cattle dealers, they took possession of the island. They built a stone walk to the island, just under water. On the island they erected a rough barn and a house with a cellar.

"They stayed there for perhaps three or five years, stealing horses, cattle and other valuable things covering a radius of fifty miles and over.

"By this time they had become quite prosperous. Their house burned down and they moved on southwest again.

"After wandering nearly three hundred miles they were all captured and killed, except one old, man when they had tried to steal corn and stock from Indians.

"This old man came back to this country and told of how the leader had buried his treasure in the stone cellar on the island, intending to return the next year.

"He told them by taking two cords and stretching them from opposite corners so that the middle of the stone cellar of the burned house could be found, then taking what he thought was

IOWA LEGENDS OF BURIED TREASURE

a point eight feet straight east from the center, then lifting out a rock and digging, the treasure could be found. He told that the cellar had been filled up with dirt, but he knew about where it was.

"After looking two weeks, searchers found the stone road. They dug out the cellar. But after following the old man's directions they still didn't dig out the treasure. Some thought the tricky old man had got them to dig out the cellar for him, then taking what he knew was the right directions, he found the treasure and left, because he came up missing shortly after the cellar had been dug out.

"Up to now no treasure has been found, although much hunting and digging has been done."

19.
Digging Children
Wilton Junction Treasure
Muscatine County

The following letter came through the courtesy of the *Wallaces' Farmer* from Mrs. Harold Brammeier of Wilton Junction, Muscatine County.

"It happened about fifteen years ago (when we were children) my brother and I had been reading 'Treasure Island,' and, of course, feeling quite excited about the treasure, we suddenly remembered having heard some time ago about gold having been buried around in that vicinity by a robber years before.

"'Let's see if we could find it,' said my brother. Needless to say I was willing, but where should we start? We lived on a farm so there were a great many places that could be used for hiding places. Talking it over we decided to start under the grape arbor, and getting our spades we began what was to be a long hard job for one of our years.

"We dug, and dug, and dug, until there was nothing unturned under the arbor, even the grape roots (which, of course, we each received a spanking for), until our backs were ready to break. But, after a night of rest and thought we were as ready as ever to start out again in the morning. Where should we dig next? There is a large rock about three feet in diameter in our yard, so I hit upon the idea that it must be under that stone, but how could it be moved? It appeared to be sunk quite a way down into the ground, so we decided to try digging around it. But, dig as we would, we could strike nothing but rock, so we had to abandon that place.

"Our next try was in our willow grove, north of the house. Beside one of the willows was a peculiar shaped stone, so moving the stone we began again. We had dug for about

Digging Children

fifteen minutes when suddenly my brother yelled 'I've struck something.' Of course, we were positive we had found the treasure, so digging a little more we were surprised to see a small tin box that was very rusty from lying in the ground. Upon opening it, imagine our disappointment in finding only rusty nails and bolts.

"By this time Father had discovered what we were doing, and this is what he said. 'If you youngsters are so anxious to dig I will see that you get plenty to do.' There is a small cave on our place, and Father had been in to make it larger, so it could be used for a sub-cellar, so, we were doomed to help dig.

"We had been digging along one side for perhaps an hour, when I struck some pieces of wood, and not being able to dig it up I called Father. So he cut and dug until he got them out, but this left quite a hollow place, as that seemed very queer we examined it. And, reaching down, Father pulled out a small chamois bag which was very heavy, and opening it found bright yellow gold nuggets. Talk about surprises, that was the biggest one we have ever had. There proved to be two bags, each amounting to several thousand dollars in money.

"Father let us each have one bag and taking it to the bank we felt like real heroes, to think that after all it was not a bluff.

      (Signed) "Mrs. Harold Brammeier"

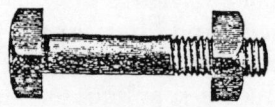

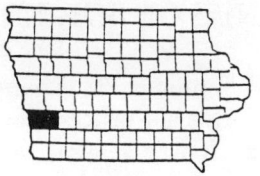

20.
Weston Bank Robbers
Weston Gold
Pottawattamie County

This story also comes as a letter through the *Wallaces' Farmer* from Archie Tye of Griswold.

"Early in the summer of 1920 the bank in Weston, Iowa, was robbed about nine a.m. one day. Weston is a small town located a few miles east of Council Bluffs on the Rock Island and Milwaukee railroads in Pottawattamie County. The robbers were dressed in overalls and drove an old Ford. They appeared to be farmers. They seemed to drop right out of sight when the banker gave the alarm. No clue could be found as to their whereabouts.

"Sometime that fall some people living in an old shack in Garner township about five miles west of Weston were being watched for thefts and moonshine. The Pisgah store had been robbed, harness had been stolen from different places so these people were being watched. One day, I think it was in November, the officers of the town swooped down upon them. They got right in the middle of a bad hornet's nest, or some other hot nest. For sometime it seemed like it might be that place where snowballs are unknown. One officer was shot to death. Some of the robbers were captured and some got away. A woman was among them and proved to be the most valuable prisoner in the bunch. She was a real actress. She acted as though to faint and asked for her husband to come to her and some way passed the gun to him that killed the officer. Well, in the cleanup they found the Pisgah store stolen goods and got from the prisoners the names of the places the other goods came from and where hidden. The old room in the loft had one window and was fixed with a rifle all loaded and an old green curtain draped around to hide it. This gang turned out to be the Weston bank robbers. But the officers couldn't get them to tell where the money was. It was several thousand dollars. They told different stories about it. One was that the robber who got away took it with him; another said they threw it away. Anyway, they didn't tell where it was. Inside of twenty-four hours, people were driving there from miles around to get souvenirs of the robbers den and to look for the money which was supposed to be hidden in that neighborhood.

A woman by the name of Mrs. Snyder owned the house and rented it to them. She didn't know them so was not implicated in the robbery. Haystacks and strawstacks were torn to pieces by treasure seekers. Some haystacks were ruined by the big holes torn out of them. The old house and barn were pretty well picked to pieces. But, no money was found. Still it seems to some that the robber who got away knows where it is and will come back for it. Mrs. King was the woman robber's name. She and the men, all but the one who got away, are serving terms in our state penitentiaries. Every now and then one can see where somebody has been digging for the stolen money. Someone might be lucky enough to find it, who knows?"

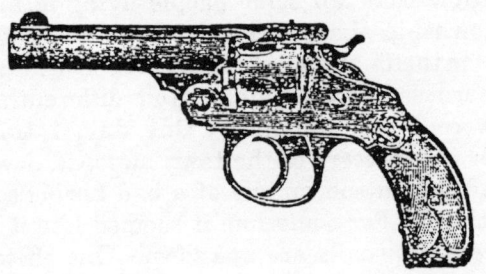

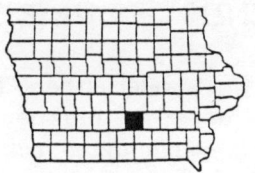

21.
Brush Creek School
Red Rock Treasure
Marion County

Beryl Pattison of Des Moines, a dabbler in most of the arts and a professional vaudeville performer, formerly lived at Red Rock where he heard the following story. He is scarcely of age.

"Somebody started up the little town of Pleasantville at a crossroads near the Brush Creek schoolhouse and a man had a jewelry store there. One night another man robbed the jewelry store. He was going along home with a sackful of things he had taken when he was overtaken by daylight or something happened so that he hid the jewelry. There was a culvert near the schoolhouse and in there he put it.

"The schoolteacher at the school then let the children do anything they wanted to and they used to run all over, down along the road and around the ditch where the culvert was. The next day after the robbery the children were playing along this ditch and went down into the culvert. They found the sack and opened it. Every little boy or girl had watches and bracelets and pearls and things and there were about forty fights over who should have what. But the two oldest boys, you know, dealt them out so many to each one and they all came trooping back to school. The jewelry man couldn't do anything about it, the things were all scattered around so and I suppose the boys all had to find out how they were made anyway.

"Some said that the jewelry the tots found was only about a third of it, that the robber had hidden it in three places for safety. Then, when part of it was found, he didn't dare get the rest of it because he was afraid people suspected him already.

IOWA LEGENDS OF BURIED TREASURE

But he wouldn't tell the jeweler either. That would have been as bad and some of the people think jewelry is just gleaming all over the place, but no one dares look for it himself, or tell anyone else where to look for fear they will be suspected of having buried the treasure and there it stays."

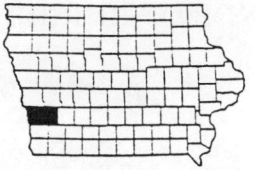

22.
Precautious as a Preacher
Honey Creek Treasure
Pottawattamie County

Jack DeWitt has already been referred to.

"You've heard about Jesse James' gold," he drawled, "up heah on Honey Creek? (Harrison County) Well, you know Jesse and the boys worked all up through this territory, jumped a train at Adel and one thing and another. They'd done a job over in Nebraska, and out across to Council Bluffs.

"Well, one of the boys had interrupted a bullet and when they made Honey Creek he was near done. Now Jesse was game to his toenails and they made camp with the posse horses snortin' at 'em and dressed the boy's wounds.

"Frank was as precautious as a preacher and while Jesse was caulking the puncture, Frank grabbed the camp kettle, filled her with the plunder and inserted her in the hillside. About that time the posse came blowing up and the bandits cut north, hellbent for Minnesota.

"They got captured and shot and one thing an' another, up there at Northfield, wasn't it? Yeah, and they never came back after that kettle of gold. She's there yet. Leastaways, the farmers think so, and I wouldn't wonder. Those boys knew how to extract."[63]

IOWA LEGENDS OF BURIED TREASURE

Jesse James from *The National Police Gazette*. Library of Congress.

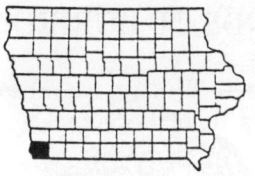

23.
Sure as Taillights on a Ford
Thurman Treasure
Fremont County

Jack DeWitt is a treasury of tales. After Jesse James he immediately swung into another trove, including this one.

"Boys," he put it, "if you want the best crack-damn treasure story I ever heard, go down to Thurman. It's down near the border and they got eva'thing down there, pots of money and skeletons and the whole show. I got some clippings on it in my scrapbook, but as I remember it, she goes like this.

"There was a rough hotel there. This was gold rush time, about forty-nine or fifty and for a couple years or so men kept driftin' in there ridin' west and they never rode no further. A bunch of hard ones ran the hotel, see, and when some fellah came along with money for an outfit, they'd either gamble it out of him or stick him in bed.

"Well, that went on awhile and there were murders enough to fill the cellar with bones, when they got a wild-ridin' two-gun sheriff. About that time they up and got law down there on the border, too. And after a coupla fights the hard ones in the hotel was all left behind or left suddenly.

"During the clean-out the hotel burned down and farmers got to diggin' around and found bones everywhere. Here about four years ago things went to boomin' again. Some fella found a pot a' gold coins, diggin' a basement for a building I think, and the country went wild. Farmers got out wheel scrapers and ripped things up generally.

IOWA LEGENDS OF BURIED TREASURE

That was at Council Bluffs. In Thurman we were told, "There's a man that's lived here two hundred years, he can tell you about it."

Michael R. Kimsey sat on a low terrace smoking a crusted brier. He looked like a small town merchant who had retired or was about to. He might have been sixty-five.

"Well, I don't know nothin' 'bout that money," he answered us. "They been diggin' a lot of course, but I don't know nothin' but what I heard."

Meanwhile, two other loungers had come up, James Torrents and a senile old man. We asked Mr. Kimsey what he had heard and with an occasional prod, which I have omitted here, he said, "Well, as I heard it, there was a bank robbery over to Riverton and it seems like one of the robbers, Polk Wells, was shot by a Riverton fellow name of Ben Ames.

"Polk lived here. I've seen him myself and he covered up his wound-like, and folks didn't know for quite a piece he was one of 'em. There was three of 'em. Seems like one of 'em got away and one was hung. Was it over to Bartlett, Jim? Do you remember?

"Well, it seems like Polk told a fellow name of Joey Campbell about the money. Yes, he'd buried it, or so he said, about $6,000, I think that was supposed to be his share, and either Joey told 'Toe-hold' Clarence or Polk told him. Maybe they was talkin' together and Clarence heard 'em. Least, Clarence told it and that was the first anybody hereabouts knew they was mixed up in it. Joey was a sort of a preacher out at a church that used to be--it's a schoolhouse now--right at the bottom of King's Hollow. Up there is where John Study, that's been doin' all the diggin' around, lives.

"Well, Polk got scared and skipped the country and they caught him, I think it was in Wisconsin somewhere and brought him back here, and then he was took up to Wisconsin again and he died up there in prison. That got 'em started and a lot of them farmers went to diggin' all over them hills. They ripped the side of one hill all up, right out in the trees, and John Study was there scrapin' around all of one summer."

He disclaimed any knowledge of the hotel with such a history as we sought.

"No, I don't know any more treasure stories less it would be the money some thinks is on the Grummins place. The place was sold awhile back for $4,000 and the money was never

Sure as Taillights on a Ford

accounted for. Folks thought it was buried on the place somewheres, but the man that owns the place don't like to have 'em dig there for it. I s'pose he thinks if it's there he'd jest as soon find it himself. Jim, here, is farmin' that place now."

Someone suggested that there must have been a lively time.

"Aw, nobody here in town got riled about them stories, but a lot of fellahs just about went wild in the country. There was old John Study, he went crazy all right. Aw, what you sayin' about him being born that way; he w'nt born no crazier 'n you were Jim, but maybe that wasn't so much."

There were a few minutes of bantering among the ancients after which we asked "Jim" if he had ever dug for the money. He was a fairly tall man, thin, with a large face on which he wore the appearance of irremovable sadness and a great deal of drooping mustache.

"No, but I purty near did once. John come to me one day and he says, 'Jim,'--you know, Mike, how he looks at you sideways--well, he says, 'Jim, I got the power to make you a rich man.' I asked him how he'd do that. I'd been up to it all my life, I says, and I hadn't found any way to fetch it. Well, he walks over to the cistern, then he walks around it a couple a' times and looked here and there and he says, 'Right here, buried about three feet under and next to that cistern, is a pot of gold and silver. There's four thousand two hundred dollars not three foot under my sole.'

"'Fine,' I says. 'Get a spade and we'll dig it up.'

"'No,' he says, 'Old Grummins wouldn't let us have it.'

"'I'll take care of Old Grummins,' I says. 'He don't need to know nuthin' about it. You git the spade and we'll divide what we find.'

"But he wouldn't do it. He seemed to think somebody over to Sidney would get him in trouble about it."

We asked if he dug later.

"Naw, if a man dug everywhere Old John told him to, he'd be diggin' ever' place. He told fellers to dig two or three places up north of here. But if you boys wants to find some buried treasure, you just go out to Old John Study. He'll tell ye. He knows the lay of every bit of buried treasure in the county and it'll be worth your while jest to see where he lives at."

At this the other villagers looked at each other. Mr. Kimsey used the voice with which he would probably prevent boys from tin-canning a dog.

"No, no, Jim. Don't send 'em out there. That ain't no place. . . ."

Jim was not to be stopped. "You go to Old John Study, boys, if you want a treasure story. It'll be worth your while. My God, it's a sight, man. You never see the like. You jest go on out there."

We went and found King's Hollow a sharp little gulch in limestone hills that fronted onto a wide plain stretching toward the Missouri River. "The second house up the Hollow" was an old and variegated shack, looking as though several very small pieces of houses had been put together. Before it, under a large tree, stood a stolid lout, chewing a homemade pipe. We asked if he were John Study.

"May be in the house, thar."

A wiry, middle-aged man came to the door. He was dressed in worn, dirty clothes including a faded flannel shirt that had once been a checker board of red and some other color. His open mouth was jagged with blackish teeth unevenly decayed and when he closed his lips one tooth--of the two that still seemed intact--thrust up past the corner of his mouth like a tusk.

I heard him say, "Damn Sunday school boys," as he slouched through the door. I told him we were gathering the old legends of the state and that we had heard of the buried treasure near there, that we did not want to dig the money but that we should appreciate his telling us the story of it. By that time another young man with a heavy countenance had come near. John looked at these two; he scowled, and his tusk crept toward his upper jaw.

"C'm'eahr, away from them fellas." He led the way to our Ford and on the far side, propped himself with a fender. "Wheahr ya from?"

We told him.

"Who telled ya this?"

We told him that also.

"DeWitt. Council Bluffs, eh? Now if I knew this fella personal, I c'd tell ya sumpthin', but bein' as is I ain't sayin'. A man got to be careful who he trusts an I'm too smart a man to let them county seat fellas get me. As far as m'self is concerned, I wouldn't care as much, but there's as fine a old man as ever lived an' he's out now an' I don't want to get nobody in. We've been in this fur some money ourselves and

Sure as Taillights on a Ford

as fur as that's concerned, alright, but I don't want to git the old man in an' we've had some particularities 'bout this afore now. If I know you fellas and knew you was alright, crack to the bottom, I c'n point you to a man's knows just where that money lays, but bein's as is, consequentially, I don't know as I got nothin' to say."

This was said disjointedly, with short pauses. We were quiet while the tusk was left guarding John's intermittent confidence. His whole manner demanded secrecy; he glanced frequently toward the two bumpkins left behind. He lifted one eyebrow or the other at intervals and nodded his head slowly in the more philosophical passages.

Now one young man sauntered toward the car. John yelled and started toward the saunterer. "You git back there. Git now!" The young man got and John slouched back to lean again on our fender.

"Mighty few men yuh can trust. I been a cowboy and I been some other things and I been into this deal, me 'n'other fella, and I ain't trustin' them guys in bus'ness like this. Prob'ly you men are in business an' you know that in business yuh're in for what yuh get out of it. If I could find a couple of fellas that's right, crack to the bottom, I could show 'em sumpthin'. Now mindja, I ain't sayin' I know where that lays. Maybe I do and maybe I don't, but I knows a old man as does know an' I got a contrack I could show ya. Got it right in that there house.

"Me an' my cousin Clarence are into this thing for five hunderd dollars, but a contrack rightin' us to dig fur sixty days, but the other side never lived up to their bargain. They's watchin' us. We seed it an' it wa'n't no use. If they's any lawin' about it, them county seat fellas'd git it all. It'd make no diff'runce if yuh found a barrel a' money if they sent some officers here from Sidney an' divvied among 'em. Money ain't no good if yuh spend your days crackin' rock. That's the way things is done in this county. Look at that road. Come a rain, can't git to town. Others in the county has good roads. We pay jest 's many taxes and they's jest 's many 'rested here as anywheres, but no roads.

"If a fella could git that money without people knowin' it, an' git out without people knowin' it, he'd be way ahead. An' I tell ya, that's the only way to git ahead. Now they's a pot full of gold some place that I could put yuh in touch with if yuh's

IOWA LEGENDS OF BURIED TREASURE

intrusted enough. It's a four-gallon brass kettle, full a' gold an' silver. Take two men to lift it. They's a wire 'round the top, smooth, just 'bout like that (he pointed to the top of a woven wire fence, about No. 10 wire) and they's a brass lid on top of it. Tween forty and eighty thousand dollars we estimated when we was diggin', an' about three an' a half foot down, below plow deep.

"We got things tore up a bit an' we seed they's goin' to play us dirt. They's watchin us, an' we left it rough there. Otherwise we'd be diggin' with teams an' scrapers yet, far's that's concerned.

But now I tell yuh, I been punchin' cattle out in Montanny afore I come here. I got two bullets through that leg, in the calf, and I got that hand shot all t' pieces so I can't double it up so. An' I got shot onct 'n the face an' I'm too smart a man to let them county seat fellas get me pickin' rocks. I knows what I knows.

"Now mindja, I ain't sayin' I can find that gold an' I ain't sayin' I can't, but they's just two ways to git it clean an another fella an' I's got into it fur five hundred dollars. Mindja I never see the gold, but it's there as sure's this here taillight's onto this Ford.

"I can take ya to the farm where it's buried, though it's been moved onct an' that's twenty-eight year ago. I don't know perzackly where it lies not it wouldn' be there, but I got my sights and my lines an' if I had the right fella to go into it crack down to the bottom an' secret, I might be able to do some guessin'. I been a purty good guesser in my time.

"Now, as I says they's two ways. We might tell the old man for a share an' I c'n take yuh to him. He wouldn't take it if it was lyin' there on the ground. He's kind of a Christian man an' thinks he ain't got the rights to what he didn't earn. If yuh give him sumpthin' it 'ud be alright. Now me an' my cousin Clarence 're ready to go alvers with the right party. We're farmin' but we'll hire hands an' put teams to the scrapers. It must 've cost us 'bout a thousan' dollars the last time, five hundred fur the contrack and another five fur the teamin' an' I c'n show ya where we cleaned the dirt away. Now 'f we c'n do this secret we don't need t' go to the ol' man atall. I might be able t'guess a lot. If Clarence 's here I'd show ya the contrack. Less go down there; maybe he's t'home. 'Tisn't but a step."

Sure as Taillights on a Ford

He led the way through brush and litter, past the remains of a buggy with alders growing through it and into an opening where a shack stood as forlornly as the first. Chickens were dusting before the threshold, but there was no other sign of life until John had opened the door a crack and asked for Clarence. A woman's voice answered.

"D'yuh know has he got that contrack here?"

"What contrack?" belligerently spoken.

"Y'know, that contrack fur diggin'."

"He did but I don't think he has now." There was some explanation which I did not hear. "Whaddya want of it?"

"They's a fella here wants to see it."

"Want's to see it? What's he want of it?"

"Well, I wanta show'im we paid five hundred dollars fur it."

"Course we paid fur it. Didn't I see it? Who says we didn't pay fur it? Where is 'e says we didn't pay fur it?"

I now saw what resembled a witch's head. She had a hawk nose and flying hair. Apparently the owner had been lying on a couch or bed, but even the dingy windows did not hide her silhouette.

I confessed my faith in the contract and edged toward the car. It looked like rain and I remembered the mud John talked about. He led us back to the Ford, allowed his protuberant tusk full extension and raised his opposite eyebrow before speaking.

"Now, I'll tell ya. See Herm McCarthy in town. He knows somethin' he might tell, but don't ya say nothin' 'bout bein' here. Me an' Herm's in on this together. Then ya see Clarence Forney. Clare's my cousin an' whatever he says ya c'n stake on. Clare's alright, crack t' the bottom, Clare is. Jest let on like ya heerd sumpin uptown. We'll take teams tomorrer an' go sharin's with the right party."

My companion asked about the money on Jim Torrents' place.

"Yeah, they's a pocketful er so there, but tain't more'n forty thousand. Thass in a old iron kettle and lays right up alongside the cistern. I c'n tell whar fifty thousan' lays along the Minawawa River outside Oklahome City, too. Ya go south out of town 'till yuh comes tuh a jog in the road crossin' a ditch an' right there its on the fur side underneath a tree to the roadside on the right. They's a clean hundred thousan' in

IOWA LEGENDS OF BURIED TREASURE

Texas, but I might not be able to find it more'n you. Somebody'll find it, though.

"Y'see, they's a bunch doin' stickin' ups all through this here country an' back in '81 they done a job in Riverton. One of 'em was winged in the leg, straight through the calf here, by a short fella in Riverton. They come this way, but they couldn't make no time on 'count of the old plug they's ridin'. They seed they's in fur it. They knowed officers wuz comin' an' they got the money buried in the forest. One got clean down Texas way, an' one took over t' Bartlett. The one that wuz winged, took 'n Minnesota, an' brought back to Sidney an' lay right over there in jail. Died in Minnesota a few year back. That's Polk Wells. Fore he died he told the old man 'bout it. Jest twenty eight year ago come August he got it out of the forest an' into a field. Thet's where 'tis right now. I go over there onct or twict a year jes' t'see they ain't no stakes put down."

I asked if the money was under a tree.

"Aw, no! They know better'n that. Too easy t'find. They buries it 'n the field, 'n' then they has their sights and their marks." I could see him sighting on a crag that fronted a hill on the east side of the valley. "That money's there, sure's that Ford of yours sets there."

The Ford was there. We got in, accepted directions to Herm McCarthy and Clarence Forney, and left. The latter gentlemen were apparently "off to a celebration somewheres."

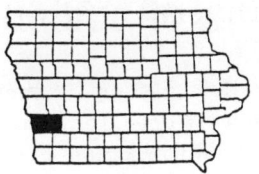

24.
A Woman Laughed
Council Bluffs Gold
Pottawattamie County

Glenn Avenue has always been close to the life of Council Bluffs. It used to start on the top of a hill where the lynchings were held and end in an impromptu plaza that fostered the watering trough. That Glenn Avenue is respectable, commercial and extensive beyond Hanger's Hill has in no way impaired its importance.

About 1880 great improvements were on and Glenn Avenue grade work progressed amiably in the company of an alien road crew, aided by heavy breaking plows. One plow jerked with thuds and rumbles through the roots of a great tree stump, when a show of gold coins were cast up. Work stopped immediately. Immigrant workers spoke a babble of many languages, scrambled over the heap of dirt, and spoke of America being the land of promise.

Local histories tell of how Muir murdered Samuels, and how "the immigrants swarmed out like bees, captured the murderer, gave him a fair trial including the benefit of clergy, attorney and a jury." After extracting a confession of the money's hiding place, the men hanged Muir and regretted it. The regret was apparently founded upon failure to find the money, not on the outcome of the lynching.[64]

Mrs. Hattie Harl also told a version of the story: "Yes, I know about the gold up Glenn Avenue. It was back during the gold rush, 1849 or '50. The Samuels boys were coming west and they picked up a man by the name of Muir, 'Baltimore' Muir. Neither bunch knew the other one, but the Samuels boys

IOWA LEGENDS OF BURIED TREASURE

had some money, about $1,500 as I remember it. When they were outfitting for the west here, they camped up on a hill east of town and one night Muir killed one of the boys for the money. The other one had gone down town. Or maybe he killed them both. At least he dispatched somebody and left with the money and a horse that he stole. It seems for some reason he didn't go far and somebody caught him. They brought him back and there is a story that he confessed to Deacon Shinn, but the deacon's own brother told me that there was nothing to that. Anyway, they put him on a mule and drove him under a limb. Then they tied him by the neck to the limb and slapped the mule on the rump. I have heard Uncle Henry DeLong tell about it. He said there was a deathly calm, as well there might have been--and when the noose tightened and he dangled there kicking, he gave out the awfullest gurgling in his throat. But that wasn't so bad as when a woman laughed, hysterically. Uncle Henry said that used to shiver his spine for years afterward. If anybody found the money they kept still about it."

There are other versions. Here is Warren Huff's.

"So far as I can tell you about Muir it was this. He was coming west with a couple of fellows he picked up east aways, and they stopped here to outfit up. A lot of them did that during the gold rush. 'Bout all that was done here then. The two he was with had $1,600 I think, or maybe it was $1,200. One night he killed one of them for it and left. The boys also had a team of horses and he took one of those and skunk out. Probably his trying to cross the river was what let them catch him.

"Now, it was this way. They found the corpse in the morning and a man named Cranall went after him on the other horse of the span. Followed him and caught him. Muir tried to hide in the brush, but the one horse nickered and the other horse answered. Muir couldn't keep the horse still and that was how they found him. They brought him back here to string him up.

"About twenty years after, a fellow--and I knowed him well--was digging for a basement. He had to dig out an old stump. Under that stump he found sixteen hundred dollars. It was in a pot of some kind, all in gold, just the way my father used to say Muir had it."

A Woman Laughed

Others say that the money was found in a secret room under the old Ocean Wave Saloon when that landmark was razed to make way for the Methodist church. There are those on the other hand who declare the saloon treasure was counterfeit Mexican dollars--mostly brass and only a little silver."

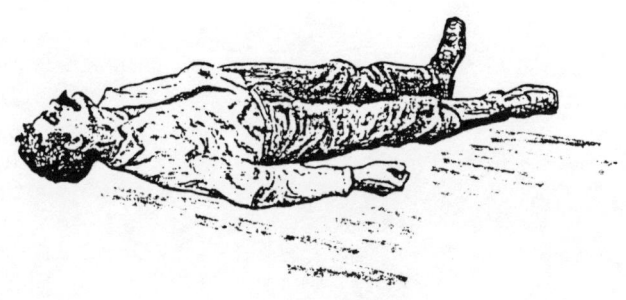

IOWA LEGENDS OF BURIED TREASURE

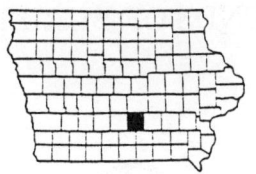

25.
Bones and Stones
Red Rock Jewels
Marion County

Beryl Pattison told me the story.

"Three or four years ago," he said, "when the graveyard at Red Rock was being extended, two men were digging a grave underneath an elm tree on the edge of the old ground. All the way down they noticed that it looked as though someone else had dug there before. There were spots of loam and spots of clay, black and yellow, as though dirt had been filled back into a hole.

"They were digging along when one of them stuck his spade right through the side of a wall. The whole side of a grave fell down. Peering in they could see a long hole and a skeleton lying in it.

"They thought it was an Indian woman because of the string of beads around its neck. The beads were of green stone and they were fastened with what they thought was a brass clasp. They were going to open the clasp when they saw that the hair was not an Indian's hair. They were afraid to dig any more in that spot, so they moved over and dug the grave somewhere else.

"When they told about finding the skeleton, everybody got to talking about it. Some of them remembered a man and a girl that had come through there about fifty years before. They had had quite a lot of money and were robbed and killed. The killers had been afraid to take the necklace because they would be identified by it if they were caught.

"Folks also thought that if the clasp had been brass, it would have been tarnished, so it must have been gold and the green stones must have been emeralds. It's still buried out there.

IOWA LEGENDS OF BURIED TREASURE

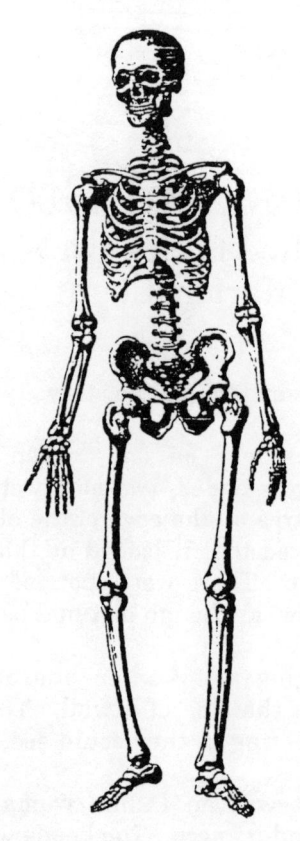

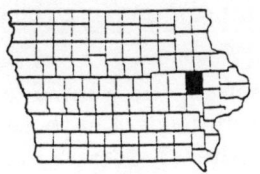

26.
Horse Thieves and Counterfeiters
Cedar Rapids Treasures
Linn County

Osgood Shepperd brought sprightliness with him when he came to Cedar Rapids in 1838 or 1839. He drove out Wilbert Stone who had made pretensions at discouraging horse thieves at his hotel. The kindred also had a shack on an island up the Cedar River. It was there presumably, that they hid the horses, secreted the harness and buried the gold that they picked up about the country.

Barthinius L. Wick, about sixty years old, lawyer and historian of Cedar Rapids, told me the following.

"I heard a story once," said Mr. Wick, "that a chance traveller came to Sheppard one night and was making fun of the country, saying it was no place to make money. Sheppard replied by reaching under the counter and bringing up gold and silver by the handful. A blacksmith east of town years back told me he knew there was money on that island. Some of those islands were swamped when they raised the dam and I guess the rest were sucked up by dredgers. The sand was used in building foundations and occasionally harness buckles and an old coin or two would sift out of the sand.

"I heard something once about money in Cuppy's Grove, and there was a story in my young days about gold back of Harper's Tavern. Bill Harper was supposed to have buried the money But he was a severe sort of person and he may have

IOWA LEGENDS OF BURIED TREASURE

started the rumors himself. He wanted to be considered rough, because rough men were leaders in those days."

As yet none of these stories has appeared in any completeness. This may be due to faulty collection or to such characters as Hiram Roberts, who is said to have taunted his lynchers with a boast. He claimed he had started more than $10,000 of spurious coin on its illicit way.

"Old Spurlock the Counterfeiter" doubtless started many a lusty legend. No evidence indicates he ever so much as passed a counterfeit dime, but he made a good living on little more than a bad reputation. He traveled about the country exhibiting new government money, insisting it was counterfeit and offering to sell more of it for fifty cents on the dollar. When the deal was completed, he took advance payment and forgot to return.[65]

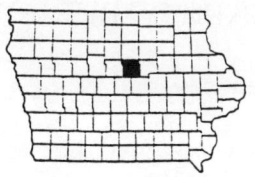

27.
Steamboat Rock
Steamboat Rock Treasures
Hardin County

There's a gold mine above Steamboat Rock, buried treasure below it, and the plunder of two notorious gangs all around it, yet the good people of Hardin County seldom dig for any of these. "The less said about it the better," they will tell you.

The Bunkers were the first of those who should have bequeathed tradition. They owned a farm and were industrious, but not inclined to agriculture. Histories tell how after years of petty thieving they were caught and on the way to Des Moines. Officers half hung one brother to jerk a confession from him. The other brother deemed this ominous and ran. The sheriff and the posse ran after him, and when they returned found the first brother understandably dead. It was then decided that equality was the basis of justice and accordingly the remaining Bunker was hanged.

On such a background, Benjamin Bowman, a stage driver now ninety-five years old and retired to Eldora, told me the following.

"I have thought," said Mr. Bowman, "the Bunkers might have buried money, but I never heard where. If they did bury it, nobody would know where. A man named Ethan Aikins from upstate New York told me of a plot to murder him for money. He was worth a half million and always carried a lot with him. He was coming west at the time and the Bunker boys had said they would buy some horses from him. The deal was practically made. He was to stop there overnight and close things up, get the money and come on into Eldora in the morning.

"Spence Garnder, a foreigner that come here and went to work for the Bunkers without knowing who they were, told me he heard men and horses coming and going all night. Maybe Aikins heard something like that. He didn't stop, just came right on through to Eldora. He told me afterward he had inquired round a little and he was sure they had laid a plot to murder him that night for his money. Course, they never bought the horses. They never bought horses from anybody. They didn't need to. But if they had robbed anybody else like that and buried the money--there was no banks then in the eighteen-forties--why, the money would have to be there. Hung the way they were, they couldn't have dug it and I suppose nobody else would know where to dig."

The Rainsbarger story stirred the community and it may be significant that a search of more than usual diligence produced only suggestions that "there might be some counterfeit money buried up along the hills somewhere."[66]

Gold was panned both north and south of Steamboat Rock. Dad Wickham made good wages building sluices and a druggist perspired his dyspepsia away, but the stories one might expect are never told.

Mr. Wickham, over seventy, still lives in Steamboat Rock. He tells the story of the mediums' treasure hunt:

"It was about fifty-five years ago, that Bob Fiskins was depot agent at Steamboat Rock. He was comin' from the depot up town--the flat was covered with hazel brush then, before any houses--and that was the last ever seen of him. He started out whittlin' a lath. When they got to looking for him the next day, they found the shavin's scattered down along the path and where they stopped, out lay the lath in the brush, but no Bob.

"Seems he must've been murdered 'cause he had money in the bank and he wouldn't hardly have left that behind if he was just leavin.' Some said he'd cashed railroad time for some fellers at the depot and the bums hangin' 'round knew it.

"A week later maybe, some fellers come from down Marengo way. They said they was mediums and they'd been talkin' with Bob, that he'd told 'em they was to come and dig him up, that he'd been murdered for the money he carried but

Steamboat Rock

that the robbers hadn't dared take the money. He said they'd just buried the body and gold and all in a sandbank down the river. They had sittin's down where the murder was s'posed to be and they went down the river and dug in some sandbars, but I never heard of 'em findin' anything."

Little evidence appeared that this or any of the other tales are often repeated. Resentment against Rainsbarger publicity and the feeling that a reputation for wildness blights the community may contribute to their stifling. There is a general feeling that the murdered Johnson and his conferees were counterfeiters and little else, that whatever they buried is worthy neither of search nor of interest.[67]

IOWA LEGENDS OF BURIED TREASURE

Part 3
TREASURES OF QUEER CHARACTERS

A few treasures which depended upon violence have provided very mild stories here. In some cases this calm would seem due to the difference between the imagined and the actual dangers, but more frequently it represents a break in the story. This break, in turn may depend either upon loss in retelling or upon faulty collection. In gathering folklore, so much depends upon finding the proper raconteur and upon breaking down reserve that omission cannot be considered of great significance, especially where the ground was scantily searched.

In the following group of legends, violence and dangerous transportation will be found still playing their parts, but the burial of money depends in a particular manner upon the character of an individual.

One of the earliest legends I can recall came from our hired man and deals with an Irishman, Michael O'Grady. O'Grady told how he was wandering home one morning after his regular Saturday night imbibing, when quite in the high road there appeared a white object at least eight feet high.

Now, Michael was no coward. He would have attacked anything from an angry bull down, and with no more than his fists. But he was more timid in matters of the spirit. He therefore felt around the road for a rock and found none while the ghost advanced upon him, towering like a sail and flapping ominous arms.

Mike's surprise at this forwardness, and the reserve provided by his liquors, aided him now. Thrusting his unprotected hand into the packed earth of the road, he probed for a rock. So great was his desire, he drove his hand ever deeper until he had plunged down the entire length of his forearm. Finding there a sufficient stone, he dispatched it with all haste at the ghost, who screamed and inspissated.

As proof that he had not been a victim to exhileration, Mike is said to have exhibited his right arm the next morning, showing it scratched and dirt-smudged to the elbow.

The story had no reference to buried money, but it was always told in connection with gold that the old man had tucked away somewhere.

Hermits are given credit for interring unusual amounts. Every year corpses engender some prospect of cash. John J. Aheurn left a jar and a can of money that were valued at more than $1,500 in Dubuque last spring.[68]

Logan, Iowa, was disturbed during the winter when a man left behind but little visible property and a rumored boast that he had $2,500 "in a good safe place all right."[69] They might be typified by G. Alfred Erickson who during the past fall started New Albin on the way toward a thrifty legend.[70] Erickson was a Swedish immigrant who saw the financial possibilities of "buying time," saving enough money to start himself in the business and then frequented the lumber camps in the winter and the harvest fields in the summer, studying the credit of employers and buying judiciously. As he made his money he invested it, and when the country was built up he owned a general store, some residential property and two lumberyards. Women did not interest him and several generous acts gave him a local name for philanthropy. If there was a church supper he insisted militantly upon paying for his entire table and if there was a launch party he provided boat, bread and beer. When he was well on in life a conservative banker said he was worth at least $100,000.

In his youth and middle age he had read much and was known as the town authority on almost everything. As he grew old, however, he turned much to himself, lost his skill in business, his conviviality, and probably most of his money. He was called "queer," attended railroad sales and bought for his store great stocks of goods that rotted on his shelves.

He was thus almost legendary before his death. When the final touch was added and the store locked pending an accounting of the estate, rumors began at once. The executor found some $20,000 in the bank and real estate would have

Treasures of Queer Characters

increased this sum, but the belief was current that at least half of the $100,000 was not accounted for. One man told of presenting a large bill and of staring while Erickson pulled a jugful of gold and silver from a recess. Another, who cashed a check after banking hours, described him picking a fruit jar of money from a convenient counter. The belief became current that the store was full of money, that ancient peas jostled jars of gold upon the shelf and that with the opening of the store, opulence would descend upon the heirs.

The store actually contained articles of variety, but not of great value. The old man didn't hide his gold in his store? Obviously, then, he hid it elsewhere. But where?

IOWA LEGENDS OF BURIED TREASURE

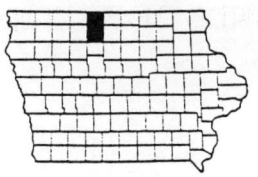

28.
No Confidence
Algona Treasure
Kossuth County

Harvey Ingham, editor of *The Des Moines Register*, over sixty years old, told the story about Doctor Cogley of Algona.

"The doctor lived south of town when I was a youngster," Mr. Ingham said. "With some reason, he had no confidence in the banks of the town and buried $2,000 in gold. As I remember it, he hid the money in a wood a short distance from his house and he was so concerned for its safety that he would walk out each evening to convince himself that it was still undisturbed. On one of these visits, he found nothing but a hole. He had been so solicitous for its welfare that he had worn a path to it. The thief needed only to follow that path which for no apparent reason had led down into the woods."

IOWA LEGENDS OF BURIED TREASURE

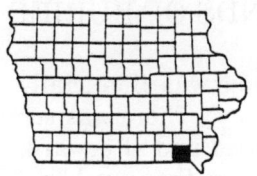

29.
A Long Slim Box
Stockport Gold
Van Buren County

Edgar R. Harlan, curator of the state museum in Des Moines, a man probably a little under fifty years of age, recounted the following. "Yes," he said, "I know of a treasure story and I can vouch for the historical accuracy of the trappings, though the treasure is legendary. I heard it when I was a youngster in the southwestern part of the state, in Van Buren County. I believed it then, all right. I've dug for that old man's money a dozen times, poking around in the stumps, turning over stones, scrambling through every ditch and probing poles through the hollow logs.

"He was the grandfather of Wilson C. Lane, I forget his name, a Carolinian, as most of the early settlers near Stockport were. For many years it was a Carolinian community. By many he was thought to have secreted money on Summer Creek. He was a little old man, living in a little old house and was by some considered a hermit and something of a miser. Across the creek he owned a rocky forty, and spent much time poking and digging around over there for no explainable reason.

"One day he was seen crossing this creek with a long slim box under his arm. It was said to be about four feet long and perhaps eight by twelve inches at the ends. When he came back he no longer carried the box and the talk was general that he had buried money over there. There was a suggestion, too, that he had buried gold at other times, for upon his death little of value was found about his shack. The belief was general that the old gentleman was financially comfortable, had he cared to live in that way. There was some digging over on his forty even before he died and afterward, whenever a bunch of boys went rabbit hunting, they would dig for the old man's box of money. There weren't any rabbits anyway.

"The only other treasure I know about was connected with a man by the name of Skee, who was cashier at a bank in Farmington. He wrote me once, saying he had a device for locating buried treasure. He wanted me to go hunting treasure with him and to divide the findings. It was some sort of electrical device, I believe, but he went down into Louisiana looking for treasure and died there. I never got my half and if death was what he got I don't know that I want it. I presume he knew of all sorts of treasure."

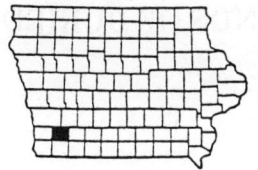

30.
Dust Over Everything
Villisca Treasure
Montgomery County

E. C. Moore, a reporter on *The Des Moines Register*, about twenty years old, told the following:

"I was raised down at Villisca in Montgomery County and there was an old fellow died down there that people thought buried a lot of money. He lived by himself, hermit stuff, you know, and never spent anything except for stale bread and scrap tobacco.

"All the old boys thought he had a lot salted away, see? Well, he died and they couldn't hardly get him buried before they started looking for his money. They found it too, but not much. There was dust all over everything about an inch thick and stuck around his shack in foolish places they found five dollar gold pieces, bills and silver, but not much. It seems people had seen him digging around in the yard, and they supposed he had been burying gold. The treasure hunters dug around but found nothing and I guess they dig there yet a little."

IOWA LEGENDS OF BURIED TREASURE

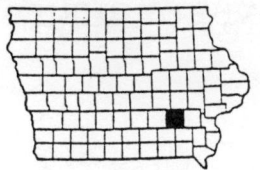

31.
Three Brothers
Hedrick Treasure
Keokuk County

This story came in a letter through the *Wallaces' Farmer* from Miss Opal Chadwick, Hedrick.

"Once upon a time during the Civil War a man and his three boys lived on a farm about twenty miles from my home at present time.

"This old man had saved a lot of money and like a lot of old men he buried it for safekeeping.

"When he found out he was going to war he told his oldest son where it was buried, for his wife had passed on when the youngest son was born.

"This brother said nothing about this story of the gold being buried to his brothers, until he was taken sick one night. He seemed to know that he would die so he called his brothers and told them the story. These two brothers tried to find the gold, but couldn't. The story got out and soon many people tried to find it. One man was said to have been dragged through a pond by a ghost. After that they never tried to find the gold.

"At the home a noise at twelve o'clock is heard. It sounds like some one is shoveling corn. People have moved there just to move away again because they can't determine what the sound is unless it is haunted by the dead brother. The corner is called 'the haunted corner.' I have heard this story repeated many times."

IOWA LEGENDS OF BURIED TREASURE

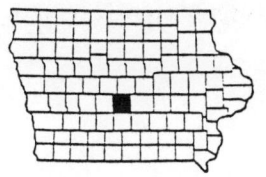

32.
They Came and Dug
Des Moines Treasure
Polk County

At Cottage Grove Place in Des Moines there is a rumor that a woman once dug for the chest of gold her eccentric father had buried in a cellar. Mrs. Dyer, 2108 Olive Street, a woman of middle age, stopped getting supper long enough to tell me about it.

"Yes," she said, "they came and dug here all right, but there won't be any more people dig, I can tell you that. It was a woman and she said her father had been killed while they lived here and I guess she did live here once all right. She thought her father had money and buried it in the cellar, but there wasn't anything to that. She thought it was in a chest, full of gold and deeds to two farms, and they dug all over the bottom of the cellar six feet deep and now the foundation of the house is falling in. They dug for a couple of weeks until we chased 'em out. There wasn't anything to it, and I don't know how I'm going to get the cellar fixed without the house falling in. It was all a stunt of the newspapers, anyhow. I finally had to chase 'em away. It was the newspaper people I had to chase away last and that's how I know that they was at the bottom of it."

IOWA LEGENDS OF BURIED TREASURE

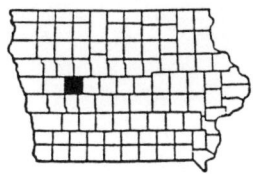

33.
Potato John
Manning Treasure
Carroll County

Elizabeth Sinn, a recent graduate of the University of Iowa, and now doing newspaper work in Des Moines, told me, "Manning had a lot of things when I was a little girl. One of them was the biggest bar in the state. There were thirteen bartenders there along two-hundred seventy-five feet of bar and none of us kids dared go down town because 'the drunk men 'd get us'. Mother used the drunk men like bogeymen and Sunday morning the farmers' wagons would still be hitched, all along the street.

"That wasn't the only funny thing about Manning. The other was Potato John, who provided our buried treasure story. He claimed, before he died--that must have been two or three years ago, maybe more--that he was one hundred and thirty years old. He might have been eighty. He was such a wizened, shrivelled little old fellow that you could hardly tell.

"He came over here from Germany when he was just a young man and he left his girl behind. He was going to go back after her when he got wealthy. She was supposed to be a tall, golden-haired girl, beautiful and above his station. While he was getting up to her station, his brother married her and that was the matter with him. He went crazy. He wasn't violent, just lived by himself out in his hut. He saved all the money he could make, kept it in gold and wouldn't put any of it in the bank.

"There were a couple of hollows that he frequented in winter. He didn't have any house in the summer, but just slept out around most any place. In the winter he would build him a shack, one of the kind made of boards with tin on, a dug place under it, a flat roof on top and a little bit of a stove inside. There was just room enough inside for the stove and for him to curl around it like a cat. There he'd stay in the night and in the day he would go off planting potatoes if it was potato season. That was why people called him Potato John.

"The little boys always tormented him when he was home and hunted through his shack--just ransacked it for his money when he was gone. Everybody knew he must have money and, of course, he would hide it around somewhere if he did. Boys would go there, pound on the tin of his shack and when he came out, they would run, just helter-skelter. When he didn't come out they would go inside and turn upside down everything they could find. In the summer they would hunt along the railroad track past his place and up and down the two gullies. Every winter he built a new shack. You would be going along over a hill, see a little smoke, and down under the brow would be Potato John's chimney fuming away. But, nobody ever found Potato John's money, although I guess they are hunting for it yet."

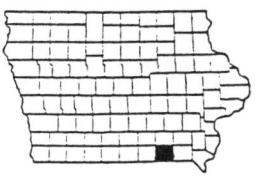

34.
Old MacDonald
Pulaski Treasure
Davis County

The following was told by the Rev. J. H. Ragan, 1360 Twenty-seventh Street, Des Moines, a retired pastor who is now about seventy-five years old.

"My folks always thought that my grandfather MacDonald who lived on a farm in Davis County buried some money. They didn't know how much, but there was more than $500 in gold that he had. Then a man had paid him some silver just before grandfather died and he had sold a horse. That wasn't much in them days, but it was something and they didn't have greenbacks then, just gold and silver. And if he buried it, right there it would be yet.

"I'll tell you the sort of man he was. His daughter, my aunt, was working with him helping build a worm fence. One of the neighbors came along and paid him some silver for something or other and he just lifted up one end of one of the rails, put the money on the rail below it and put the rail back. Right there he left the money--quite a piece, I think--at least until they needed some money. Then he sent my aunt down after it.

"When he got old he came to the house one day and got the ax and the grub hoe. He had treed a mink, he said, and he wanted to hole him. Back he went down into the woods and he didn't say anything more about getting the mink or not getting it and about six months after that he died. The folks looked for his $500 in gold and they couldn't find it. And they didn't find the money he got for the horse.

"Things went along for awhile. Then one day came an uncle of mine by marriage and says to my aunt, says he,

'Your brother' (that was my uncle and his brother-in-law) 'is lyin' a-sick of the tuberculosis and is like to die, but he wouldn't take no rest until I'd come up here and looked for that $500. He dreamt three nights hand running that that money was buried down here in the woods under a certain tree and he says to me, "Before I die, I want you should look for it."'

"There he'd been down there looking for it, but he hadn't found nothing. We went and looked too, and from the dream as he had it, we picked out a certain white oak that we thought ought to just about be it, but we didn't find anything. He didn't either, or if he did he didn't say anything. Whether he would if he'd found it I couldn't say."

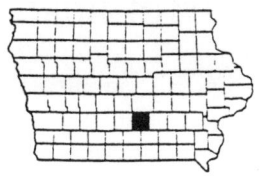

35.
Schoolhouse Floor
Brush Creek Treasure
Marion County

Beryl Pattison of Des Moines told the following story of Brush Creek Treasure.

"He was a bachelor and I think he had some money when he came out here fifty, sixty, seventy years ago. He lived off by himself in the woods by Brush Creek in Marion County. And you know, he wouldn't spend much so he saved quite a lot. After while, two or three people were robbed near there--quite a ways away too, ten or fifteen miles. And he thought maybe they were going to rob him.

"Things went along for a week and one night he felt queer. He thought surely he would be robbed that night, so he got out all his money. Then he took a crock or kettle that he had, just something he used about the fireplace, and wrapped the money up in that. Then he walked so many paces in this direction and so many in that--you know the way they do--and then some more in another direction and at last he buried the money. Sure enough the robbers did come that night and tried to get him to tell where the money was. He wouldn't tell. And so they shot him or stabbed him or put him out of the way somehow. Then they burned his cabin and maybe him in it.

"Now, how this got out I don't know, unless the robbers themselves told it, but after while two men came down from Des Moines and they paced all over. By this time a schoolhouse had been built right where the old man's cabin used to be and they dug all around there. They said they found a rock with the directions on and they pulled up the plank of the schoolhouse floor and they poked around the foundations because they thought that the marks on the stone meant that the gold was buried where the schoolhouse had been built. But they couldn't find anything. Then about fifteen years ago the schoolhouse burned and people dug a lot more, but they didn't find anything."

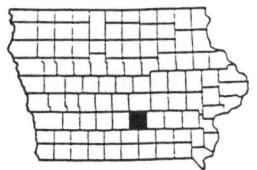

36.
Terribly, Terribly Drunk
Dunreath Treasure
Marion County

Beryl Pattison also gave me this story.

"He was an important man in one of the banks in Dunreath. I think he was the cashier or the president of it and one night he went out and got just terribly, terribly drunk. When he was going home, in the condition he was, he thought someone was going to rob the bank. He went in and took all the money (out of his cash drawer) thinking he would take it home with him, carrying it in his pockets and his hat.

"He lived on the edge of town and when he got out there he thought somebody would be coming after him there, too. So, he kept going along. He went into a forest where he kept falling over sticks and rocks and ruts and roots. Every time he would fall down he would be afraid that he had spilled some of the money. He thought now no one would follow him into the forest, so he might as well hide the gold. He fumbled around in the hollow of an old tree and left the money there. After that he went home to bed.

"The next morning he couldn't remember much about it. He knew he had thought a lot of things the night before. He went down to the bank and found a lot of people and a great to-do there because the money was gone. He didn't say anything because he didn't really know how much of it had happened. He helped hunt just like the rest of them. He took a couple of long walks, too, and thought if he had spilled the money he would find some of it, but he couldn't find any of it. He couldn't be sure where he went nor what kind of a hollow tree he had put it in. No, they never did find the money. The story has been in our family a long while, but I don't know how it got there unless he got happy again and told it on himself.

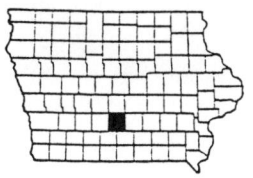

37.
Dead Ringer
Dunreath Ring
Marion County

Beryl Pattison also told this:

"Bill Cowman lived eight or ten miles out of Dunreath. He came there when the country was young and he never married. I don't know how much he had, but he had whatever a bachelor has who lived alone all his life, worked hard and saved his money. Fifty years ago he came, when the country was young. When he got along in years he had a lot of heirs by his relatives. It seemed to him as though he saw they were just sitting around waiting for him to die and not doing much else in the meantime.

"Old Bill didn't like that, but he didn't say anything either. He didn't pay much attention to his relatives anyway, so that wasn't so surprising. His best friend was one of the neighbor women, although there wasn't anything wrong about that whether she was married or not. He simply liked her as a good friend and she apparently liked him and that's all there was to that. Then he got sick and she took care of him.

"Right here in the story is where he ought to die, you know, and leave her all his money. But, Old Bill didn't do that. He had cancer and he knew he was going to die, but he didn't make any will. Instead he had the woman go to town and talk things over with the doctor and the undertaker. He didn't have any other bills around anywhere, but he found out what his doctor's bill was going to be and how much it would take to have himself buried. He arranged for the grave and the tombstone and, by the way, bought the cheapest one they had.

"He gave his woman friend enough to pay all the bills and a little to see to it that his grave was looked after. He wanted everything done respectable, but he didn't seem to care much how and then he took all the rest of his money and gave that to the woman, too.

"The money he gave her wasn't for her to keep, though, as the neighbors found out after she had got back from her trip to the East. The heirs found it out, too. He had told the woman to buy him the best ring that could be bought for whatever money was left and when she got back with it, he put it on and just waited around to die.

"Everybody was waiting for Old Bill to die, then, and he finally did it. He had told the woman to make sure the ring was on his finger and leave it there. They did and that's the way they buried him.

"The heirs didn't make much fuss about his grave. They fussed when the ring went into it out of sight, but when Old Bill was once inside and the ring along with him, nobody seemed so much interested in Old Bill. Some talked a lot about the ring and wondered if the grave wouldn't be dug open, but I could never see that it was. His woman friend married a man from the East and moved away. His grave looks now as though Old Bill didn't have any friends at all anymore and he took everything else he had with him, from his ring down to his jackknife. He made them put those things in the coffin too. I almost forgot that."

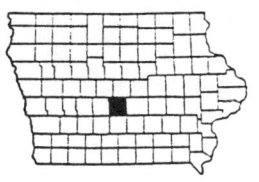

38.
Rags
Rising Sun Treasures
Polk County

Old Tom Bidwell--some called him "Rags" because of his profession--was probably the William Morris among those who buried Iowa treasure. The practice was a daily affair and almost an art with him. Had he left no rumors of unrecovered gold he would have been as unnatural as a childless Don Juan. His brothers, farmers forty-five or fifty years old, live on the home place north of Rising Sun.

"I don't mind tellin' ya," George conceded, "but we always figgered we'd find that gold ourselves. Some of it anyhow. It's buried out here in the cornfield all right. Sure ya ain't goin' to do no diggin'?
"Yes, Tom buried money. I've seen him lots of times."
"No, you ain't, volunteered Frank. "Nobody couldn't see him when he buried money. I've watched him. I couldn't see him er nobody couldn't. He'd have the money and he'd make a kind of a sweep (with a gesture) 'n' then he didn't have it. Seems like he was jest too quick fer ya. Quicker'n lightnin' he was. I've seen him many a time. Think I c'd find that money? No, sir! He could, though. He knew right whar t' look. I want t' tell ya."
"Casionally he didn't," George continued. "They's that cornfield money, now. He buried that near a corn hill an' a fence post. My sister seen him when he done it, right outa that there back window. He was gone workin' after that. He worked all over this country and buried money ev'ry place he's a hand, an' some places he wasn't. We didn't know he'd buried the money 'counta' him bein' so quick an' he couldn't

never find that money. He musta' dug nigh two weeks. How much was they? 'Bout three hunderd dollars, he claimed. My sister seen him bury that money an' she dug too, but she couldn't find it no more'n him. If he couldn't find it nobody could, I guess. No, we ain't dug much. Oh, we dug some, but I always figgered we'd plow that money out some time. I plow special along there.

"Like's not they's money buried 'round here most anywheres 'f a feller knew where t' look. Tom went out t' Calliforney 'n the gold rush a' '49. That's where he learned to bury money. Them miners all buries it. He had quarter-share in a mine till he got beat out a' it. I al'ays figgered he buried money in Minnesoty, too. He died up there 'bout ten years back. He never made no confession or left no papers as we could find.

"Ya better see George MacFadden--lives over to Prairie Center," Frank volunteered. "Him an' Tom had a fight onct 'bout some buried treasure. George driv' him off the place. Tom'd been aworkin' fer him, an' he buried some money 'n George wouldn't let him dig fer it."

Mr. MacFadden is older, perhaps seventy and a retired farmer.

"Yes, I suppose I can tell you as much about Old Tom as anybody. Nobody knew much. He came and went as he pleased. Yes, I've seen him bury money, much as a hundred times, I suppose. He din't believe in banks, so he had to bury it. Always got money in gold and silver and hid it, some here and some there. He always carried quite a little with him and while he was workin' he'd bury it near an oat shock or a fence post. He used to tell me sometimes where it was, but I don't think he told the men.

"The only funny story I can think of about him happened at my old place. He was sleeping in the icehouse. It was cool and soft. He wan't very clean sometimes, had queer eating habits--he was a bachelor you know--and he would pick up what he found, scraps of meat and the like, and carry them in his pocket.

"Well, one morning he came to me and he'd been robbed. He wouldn't have it no other way. He dug around the icehouse awhile and he found his wallet jammed down into a rat hole. I

Rags

s'pose some rat was after the grease on it. He 'bout dug up my carriage room floor once.

"Nuther time, and that was about the limit, he dug for some money in the orchard. I didn't mind much what he did, but I didn't like to have him shovel off the whole farm. He must've been at it three weeks, shovelling the dirt through a sand screen. He said he buried a hundred dollars there, but I had to tell him I thought he'd dug enough. He was digging the whole orchard full of holes and dirt hills. He din't want to stop at first."

Mrs. I. E. Proudfoot lives about half way between Prairie Center and Des Moines on a modern farm. She is yet too young to be termed middle aged.

"The only treasure I know about," she laughed, "is the one that Rags buried under our hedge. The hedge isn't there any more, but it used to run from the corner of our house right down to the road.

"This was a convenient half-way point for him on his trips to Des Moines. He had a horse and a sort of old wagon, you know, and most any morning we'd wake up and see the horse tied to the wagon. That meant Rags was asleep in the barn. One day he asked for a pitchfork and went digging around down there most of the forenoon. When he came up he was crying, just about. I know how sorry I felt for him. I was a little girl then. He said he had buried a can full of gold under that Osage orange hedge. You know how prickly they are, all spines. He thought it would be all right there if it would anywhere, but he knew somebody had taken it. And we didn't find it either. There had been a man trim that hedge about a week before. I don't know that Rags buried money under that hedge at all--people said he buried it most everywhere--but I am perfectly confident that he thought he did."

IOWA LEGENDS OF BURIED TREASURE

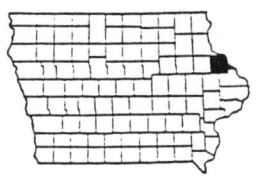

39.
Burn the River
Dubuque Treasure
Dubuque County

Iowa's first productive mines were those that yielded lead at Dubuque. Julien Dubuque was given the right to work these mines in 1778 [1788] and their operation continued until shortly after his death at the mines in 1810. Mining was revived again as soon as whites were allowed back in the territory after the Indian treaty of 1833. The miners who operated these mines had their eccentricities, considerable wealth, and no banks.[71]

"Scair-nail Dutchy" (George Scholtz, about sixty years old) told me the first of the legends of miners' gold.

He was a clammer and in the world's budget his rent must have been charged to the Mississippi River, where his houseboat sounded the wave lappings. He himself was short and his wide, whiskered face gave more evidence for the latter part of his nickname than did his accent. For the "Scar-nail," a threshing machine was said to account.

"I ain't never hunted no treasure up there, but they's the felluhs that has." He looked at the jutting, wooded bluffs. "The treasures I gets I gets out a' the river yonder. I 'member they telled me. You want to hear it, huh? You want 'o dig a little yourself, maybe? You don't? He-ah! I knows what I thinks. But I tell you anyway.

"They was this Joolian Dubuque. You heard of him? He come here early, many years early, and dig in the mines. He get the mines from these Indians and he do a lot of funny business to scare dem. One time, they tells, he pour a whole barrel oil ona creek. Then he tell the Indjians, 'You do what I say, yes? No! I burn up the river.' Then he scratch a match and throw it in and 'whoosh!' That scare the Indjians plenty.

"Now, I tell you. He buy those mines from the king of Spains and he buy dem from the Indjians, scaring dem and funny things, and he sell the lead down the river and make lots of moneys. But what good it do? He got no wifes, no places atall to spend his moneys. So, what good was it? No good at all but to bury and that is what he did with it all over those hills somewhere. That's what they tell me. I? I never dig, no, but others, they digs with shovels and they hunts with gold finder sticks and lots of things, I guess. But if I find it, mybe I have too much."

Of the later miners, Kelly is favored of legendarians. "In 1861 there was found in the old Kelly cabin, $4,000 in gold; later a boy in kicking over a tin can at the cabin uncovered $1,800 in gold; search revealed $1,500 more in an old tea canister. These discoveries caused a thorough search to be made, but no more gold was found. The search, however, led to the discovery of lead ore in the old Kelly mines."[72]

"Of course, there were stories about Kelly's cabin and Kelly's mine being haunted," Mr. Richard Harman remarked. He is a furniture dealer and amateur collector, a painter for pleasure and the author of a history of Julien Dubuque. He is now about seventy.

"There wasn't anything to the ghost stories. Old Kelly was just like a lot of other miners. They were a rough and tumble bunch, good-hearted and rough, but what did they want of money? They wanted food, powder, tools, a roof over their heads. Kelly used to keep his money in cans, and I suppose when he wanted some he would go to a can and get what he needed and in time he probably forgot about some of the cans.

"Then with time some kid would find a coin, looking like copper with age. He would bring it down and somebody would say, 'Why, that's old. Where'd you find that? Of course the kid would tell him and then the hunt would be on. It was actual enough that there were a good many finds, most of them small, but some of them amounting to several thousand dollars. There may be more there; I believe people hunt some yet."

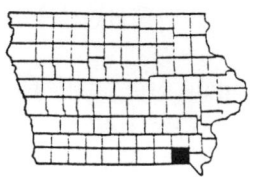

40.
Dream Tree
Stockport Treasures
Van Buren County

The following came through the courtesy of the *Wallaces' Farmer* from C. M. Still of Stockport.

"This is a true story of what happened a long time ago, but is still fresh in my mind, except dates and the exact amount of money in the kettle that John, the eldest brother, found and the amount those colored people gave him. John has been dead several years. Jess has been in California a good many years and I do not know of but one man except myself that knows anything about this."

Here the story begins: "I am a Reader of your paper and today I noticed you asked for stories of Buried Treasure in Iowa. I never had wrote anything for a paper in my life. I am sixty year old. But I will try and tell about an instance I knew of that happened in Van Buren Co., near Bonapart[e] on the Des Moines River in Van Buren County. The time, as near as I can remember was in 1877 or 1878. Two brothers were working at carpenter work and they were sleeping together on Friday night. They each dreamed of buried treasure. The oldest brother dreamed of finding a kettle of gold on a colored man's place about three miles below Bonapart[e]. On Sunday he went to the place to see if he could find the tree by which he dug up a kettle of gold in his dream. He had never been in the pasture only in his dream. But he knew where the colored man lived and when he went in to the pasture he soon found the tree he had seen in his dream. The husband and father had been killed some years before this time. The widow and two sons still lived on the place, so this man went to the house to see if they would consent to him digging for gold. He told them his dream and then the widow said, 'Lore Chile, that is where the old man done buried that gold and that mule done kick him and killed him so quick he couldn't tell us where he bury that gold.

"So, they dug by that tree and found the kettle with several hundred dollars in gold. I do not remember just how much he told me. But that was the best days work he ever done for they divided the money with him.

"And now, for the younger brother's dream. They were both sleeping in the same bed. When they dreamed these dreams the same night in the younger man's dream a skeleton opened their room door and came walking up to the bed. And he was scared so bad he could not move. The skeleton said to him, 'Young man don't be scared. I will not hurt you. But if you will go with me I will show you where you can get a brass kettle full of gold. I was traveling on the old Santa Fe Trail and camped for the night and I buried a kettle of gold. That night the Indians killed me before morning, so the kettle of gold is there yet. If you will go with me I will show you where to dig for it so the young man in his dream went with the skeleton and it led him to an oak tree on the farm of a man that some time later became the father-in-law of the young man. The skeleton told him there was three ax marks on the northeast side of the oak tree and sixteen steps northeast of the tree the kettle was buried. It was about twenty feet east of the old Santa Fe Trail from the Des Moines River to this farm and when he came to this place it looked just like it did in his dream, only the ax marks did not show on the tree. But everything else--the trail, the tree, the lay of the land and all. Time went on, this young man married the girl and her father told him to suit himself for he said it will be yours when mother and I are gone. So he done as the old man asked. Now this timber claim had never been fenced. So, after he was married, he fenced this land and cleared the brush and small trees off, but let this oak tree that the skeleton showed him stand out alone.

"And one night some years later, he had a boy staying with him and also a hired man working for him. This man's name was Jess. His hired man was Charley and the boy was Dave. Charlie was at the barn choring east of the house. Dave was after the cows west of the house. Jess and Dave were going to milk the cows. But when Jess came to the cow lot, Dave and the cows were not there and it was not quite dark. Now this oak

Dream Tree

tree by the kettle of gold stood just over a little creek south from the cow lot and Jess saw a light going round and round the tree and wondered what Dave was doing with the lantern. He could not see Dave, just the light. So, he called to Dave and Dave answered him, not from the tree, but away northeast of where Jess stood. And still the light was going round the tree. He watched it and soon the light drifted off down the creek until it went out of sight. When Jess and Dave came to the house, Charlie was there and he asked Jess what he was going round that oak tree with the lantern for. He had seen the light and thought it was the light from the barn and Jess told him he had not had any lantern. Dave had also seen the light and thought it was Jess.

"Now it comes to what I know about what came later. Jess never had courage to dig for the kettle of gold. I moved on a farm adjoining this farm where this happened. And while I lived there the oak tree died, so I told Jess if he would cut the oak tree I would help him for I wanted to see if those ax marks would show in the wood. When we split the tree open we found the three ax marks away in on the northeast side of the tree just as the skeleton told him about, but to this day the kettle has never been dug up and it is thirty-six years since I helped Jess cut that oak tree. But I still believe the gold is there. I told Jess I would help him dig, but he was afraid they would make fun of him. Jess has been gone a good many years. But I would still help the man that owns the place if he would dig. I can still go to the spot where the oak tree stood. This is a true story."

IOWA LEGENDS OF BURIED TREASURE

Appendix

The burier of treasure consciously confronts the dilemma pronged with safety and secrecy. How can treasure be guarded? How can it be marked so that its tokens appear natural? Against the first problem, myth-makers provided combustible dragons[73] and curses quite as effective. Pirates[74] were fond of murdering one of their number that a spirit of local power be provided. Later peoples have taken natural objects as the guides to treasure, thus maintaining the appearance of normalcy, but whether the feeling for the enlisting of spirits has in any measure influenced the selection of these natural symbols is a problem too involved to warrant more than suggestion.

Spirits seem everywhere to assume treasure. The Phoenix visits only those parts of China preserving it.[75] Near Greenville, Illinois, pioneer and Indian spirits are said to mingle screams over a barrel of bullion.[76] South of the Mason-Dixon line most ghosts have now found a comfortable basement to live in and convenient treasures to ward[77] and in days past West India shades were said to whisk treasure from beneath honest pirates' shovels.[78] Ghosts on the Isle of Skye are so active that natives dare not dig for the pirate hordes,[79] and pots of gold in Kincardinshire are warded by a voice that is said to shout, "The kirk and manse are on fire" and during the digger's confusion, dispose of his landmarks.[80] The shade of an American Indian cursed silver into worthless metallic lumps when his murderer mined the ore.[81] That there is something mysterious about the precious metals may be inferred from the aid given the seeker in India by the blood of a black cock,[82] and from the necessity in Japan of appeasing the bereft spirit with rice cake and of deceiving him with fake money.[83] Gold and silver bullets have always been efficacious, having disposed, among others, of Ibsen's Brand in the play by that name and of the titular Emperor Jones of Eugene O'Neill. The metals also assure success in matrimony, architecture, medicine and numberless other ventures.[84]

From ghosts there is but slight transfer to guardians having a quaint, humorous, or monstrous nature. The gold in the upper valley of the Tiber River awaits the proper person with a plate of "maccharoni,"[85] and in the Isle of Wight a tree that could only be uprooted by twelve white oxen remained immovable; some say it objected to one ox's lone black hair, and that the treasure beneath it is forever lost.[86] In Western Ireland a dog may crouch under a white thorn bush and above a great treasure, and if so he can be propitiated with a foal.[87] Tradition says a bell will attract the proper golden-haired youth to Merlin's golden cauldron at Medgelert, Wales,[88] and that above Langybi in the same land a rock stubborn to men and beasts revealed a treasure at a girl's touch.[89]

The treasure of Cardona in Spain requires of its finder interest in the manuscripts pertaining to the Cid, ingenuity at deciphering a code and sanctity before an altar.[90] Legend tells of the treasure chest of the giants of Stokesay lying under the moat of Warren Castle, guarded by ravens[91] and of a pot of gold in Breffny warded by a great cat,[92] and in Central America of winding stairways and a mysterious gold hand holding the greedy from bars of virgin gold.[93] There is also a story of a delver at Grand Pre who lost a post of Spanish gold when he thrust an instrument through the dead watcher's skull and accordingly brought a bolt of lightning, loud thunder and a strong wind that upset the digger and blew out his light.[94] In Hereczvara, black giants guard the treasure casks of the dwarfs and two black goats stand above the horde of a giant king in Kis-Borosnyo.[95] The Bedouins believe Solomon left a host of genii[96] to guard his gold, but in Chihuahua "the weeping woman" has been effective enough to make the strongest tremble.[97]

Some treasures seem sufficient to tempt the attention of the devil himself. The cauldron of treasure in Schoharie County, New York was lost when no minister would "lend himself to sorcery" with a prayer over the pit.[98] Edward, the Confessor, being equipped with second sight, mentioned seeing a black, goat-like devil bestride a barrel of tribute.[99] And it is said a

Appendix

wagon of gold on a Piedmont mountain top has attracted the shadow of shadow permanently.[100] A symposium would indicate that the devil at a breach of the diggers' code is also liable to fly off with almost any treasure "leaving behind him only panic and a strong smell of brimstone."[101]

Obstinate seekers may sometimes win treasure from ghosts and even from devils. Small devils drove one treasure hunter from Mujmbly Hill, Hungary, but the same pests showed uncounted wealth to one whom they could not outface.[102] A genial ghost at Teermichrain Castle, County Claire, Ireland, endeavored to show a timid man a treasure and was so disgusted at the human's flight that he forsook the haunt.[103] Headless pallbearers have been troublesome until allowed to reveal treasures.[104] The Magyar Jack Dreadnought bullied a ghost in strange forms and received vats of copper, silver and gold, an innkeeper's daughter and the promised absence of the ghost.[105] In Herefordshire[106] or in some of our southern states,[107] any ghost accosted with sufficient vigor must either flee or reveal treasure. Fairies who buried a "steen" (earthen pan) of gold at Bury's Ditch, Shropshire, obligingly left a gold wire exposed and leading to it.[108] In the latter territory you may recover lost money by kissing a black person,[109] money in general by throwing properly prepared cancelled postage stamps out the back window,[110] and a bag of gold by "stamping" one hundred white horses.[111] Many are the tales of those who have found treasure by following dream directions,[112] but in Macedonia, unless the dream is kept secret, the gold turns to coals.[113] In Italy the finding of treasure is reserved for him who has "racked his brains" and "learned magic."[114]

The ghostly and indicative light in the New Albin and Stockport treasures is perhaps the most usable lore in the Iowa legends included here. The phenomenon is unusual in treasure lore, and although far from unknown, there has been little if any discussion. It may therefore be appropriate to suggest an association of gold with the color of the sun and thus to light, or to the fruitfulness of riches and of light; and to investigate the lights as evidence of ghostly watchers-over or seekers-after the treasure. According to Herodotus, the Scythians traced their line of kings from a younger brother, whose divine right was indicated by gold in the shape of a plough, a yoke, a sword and a flask which descended from heaven and burned until the third brother approached them.[115] Flaming silver is said to have helped the Emperor Servius mint spurious coins.[116] A horse from whose head light gleamed all over Czechoslavakia was storied as the source of plenty there,[117] and to the Basque people the purple "Arguiduna" was guide and defender.[118] Indians advised Columbus to fast and pray before seeking gold, which was sacred and mystic,[119] and the Hindus refuse to wear gold on the feet, believing that as the emblem of the sun it must not be debased.[120]

Money buried during an attack upon a smelter on the St. Maurice River, Canada, has never been found and the lights seen playing over the ground are locally interpreted as the shades of the old governor and his retinue, hunting for the treasure.[121]

The ruddy carbuncle on Mount Washington and the flashing Diamond of Blomidon on the crags above the Basin of Minas[122] advertise themselves widely and the Beowulf treasure has retained some luminous qualities.[123] In Cornwall, the lights of "knockers," ghosts of the Jews who crucified Jesus, are followed for rich lead veins,[124] but following a Jack O'Lantern is either good[125] or bad[126] luck. In Bohemia peasants believe that a blue light hovers over buried gold, but that it is visible only to the destined finder,[127] and according to the "Skatter i Sabybaker" in Hofberg's Svenska Folksagner, "a carriage full of gold and silver is said to be sunk mid-stream, over which a weird light flickers,"[128] Grettir the Strong saw "a great burst of fire out on a ness."[129]

In Scandinavia, also, a light is indicative of the ghoul, who runs between the legs of unwary treasure diggers, splitting them laterally with his razor-like back.[130]

We are assured Pope Silvester the Second found a treasure vault under Constantinople which was lighted by a great carbuncle, putting out its light and forcing the pope to retire.[131]

In Texas a treasure seeker followed a light down what might have been a well and turned the proper stone on its rock floor. Such fire flamed from it that the treasure hunter fled while behind him was the roar of galloping horses and of fighting men.[132]

Appendix

It will be noticed that while divinatory lights are related to many peoples, the purer treasure light exhibits a strong Teutonic affinity. The Meyer family connected with the Black Hawk gold is German. To find so safe a suggestion for the Carolinians of Stockport would be more difficult. Adducing connection with the treasure guardian for other trappings of interment would seem to be an even more hazardous venture. It may be of interest, however, to note that of the thirty to forty-five[133] Iowa treasures mentioned, approximately half are not located; twelve are marked by trees, six by hills or mounds, six by rivers, wells or springs, five by stones and four by caves; eleven of the hordes are deposited in kettles, and single deposits are kept in kegs, pans, boxes and bottles. Each of these articles is so natural to its purpose that analogues are restricted to those having an especial Iowa interest.

Facility at producing kettles, a skill displayed by nomadic horse thieves, beleaguered messengers and errant bank robbers not otherwise concerned with domesticity, is at first a matter for wonder, but although cauldrons were neither light nor wieldy, kitchen utensils were the only permanent and readily available containers. Chests received the larger and especially the marine treasurers, but crocks and kettles are doubtless the most popular containers. The gold at the end of the rainbow is so encased and the Leprechauns and Clurichauns have so seeded Ireland[134] that peasants are perpetually dreaming of them to their profit,[135] or finding them under the hearthstone.[136]

If this function of kettles has any significance one would think of witches' fondness for kettles, of the Irish healing kettle and of the Scandinavian mythological kettle. The Cree Indians of Saskatchewan were said to feed from an inexhaustible pot[137] and such vessels have of course long been sacred.[138]

Tree worship would seem to be nearly universal. That the oak tree appears so frequently as an Iowa treasure marker is probably not traceable so much to its hospitality to spirits as to its reputation for stability, its frequency and its familiarity.[139] That the oak tree is unusually potent, however, cannot be denied. Some believe that when an oak falls the spirit within it groans[140] and the Mono Indians considered it ancestral.[141] Oaks have been considered most sacred in the Holy Land.[142] Their association with the druids is well known and the properties attributed by folk medicine to oak trees are unusually startling.[143] Grimm early pointed out that in folklore trees represent both home and temple[144] and Burns attributes striking anthropomorphic qualities to them.[145]

Much treasure has been buried in or near water. It may be significant that natives of India attribute the chinking of coins at night to "somebody's treasure . . . flying away to the water." In connection with the Eddyville treasure it may be of interest to note gold in Haskell County, Texas, marked by "the large bone of some prehistoric animal"[146] and remembering the Fort Crawford treasure to note that the accursed Santa Anna gold lies "on the top of a hill under a flat rock."[147] An unpublished letter gives directions for finding the Indian treasure in the hills southwest of Emporia, Kansas, by following arrow heads in Pilot Mound.[148] Stones play a strange part in buried treasure, and Lange attaches unusual significance to North American stone lore.[149]

Gold at the bottom of Lake Quatavita, Columbia, is protected by mud that solidifies on exposure to the air.[150] In Anglesey the ancient gold that King Arthur took from the Goidels is stored, guarded by a circle of stones and their ghostly powers.[151] An Ipswich legend tells of a man who moved the stone covering treasure and looked up to behold an army of black cats who answered his "seat" with a pit full of water that nearly drowned him.[152] An Irishman moved a millstone while digging dream treasure and "the mill fell down on himself."[153] Two men who sought treasure under a stone in Middleston, England, told of seeing it rise to emit a white creature that "flaffered and flew."[154] There are stories of treasure beneath the Merlin stone at Chetsey, Surrey; a "valuable treasure" at Tamlenchar Cross, Selkirkshire under a stone; a three-sided figure full of gold beneath a stone at Medon, and more under the three stones "like a cockit hat" under Kelse bridge.[155]

Raynard the Fox[156] hid his "seuen waynes . . . of syleur and of gold" under three stones. Rock often cannot be dissociated from hilltops, which are apparently favorite treasure haunts. The Cora pueblos go to "the richest mountain the ancient people know of and bargain for gold and goods

Appendix

with the master of the mountain." They pay in human lives, delivering the tribute painlessly by natural magic.[157]

The treasure of Bill Skeeters has so intrigued Oklahoma people that some are said to have become impoverished searching that plateau of the Wichita Mountains marked by certain stones.[158]

In connection with the Fort Atkinson-Fort Crawford road and its treasure it may be well to mention the Indian road from Mexico City to Pike's Peak, which gave rise to legends of golden temples on the mountain.[159] Caves have always been the home of dragon treasures, but there were very good practical reasons for the use of caves by horse thieves.

Some mention should be made of the divining rod, although the subject is elsewhere[160] so thoroughly treated that scant attention should suffice.

Prophet Smith of the Mormons was said to be a "semi-literate man who had attained some fame as one who could locate wells and hidden treasures by means of witch hazels.[161] The divining rods used to hunt the Black Hawk gold were straight sticks. Forked twigs are usually used, the holder grasping either prong of the branched end. Hazel would appear the favorite wood, and in countries where it is little known, willow, peach, apple, rowan, bamboo, alder and a dozen more seem as effective. Other treasures were sought by needles manufactured to capitalize the superstition. The trust placed in rods may be inferred from the following apparently serious quotation: "It is a fact that some of the most productive wells in the oil regions were located in this manner. It is a further fact that from time to time, search for buried treasure has been carried on in precisely this way.[162]

IOWA LEGENDS OF BURIED TREASURE

Endnotes

INTRODUCTION

1. William H. Prescott, *The Conquest of Peru*, I (Philadelphia: n.p., n.d.) p. 418 ff.
2. e.g., D. L. R. Lorimer and E. O., *Persian Tales* (London: Macmillan, 1919). The book is full of treasure, but none is left in the ground; see also Oliver Elton, trans., II, *The First Nine Books of Danish History*, by Saxo Grammaticus (London: Folk-Lore, 1893)p. 55 ff.; L. A. Magnus, *The Heroic Ballads of Russia*, (London: Kegan, 1921) p. 44. Ilya Muromets, a Russian Cuchulain, "found great caves filled with jewels and silver and gold which belonged to the fair and deceitful maiden, but he devoted all his gold and silver to God's church, and to the orphans, and so he escaped wealth and returned to the city of Kiev."
3. Ralph Delahaye Paine, *The Book of Buried Treasure*. (New York: Sturgis, 1911) p. 14.
4. Washington Irving, "The Legend of the Death of Don Alonzo de Aquilar," *The Alhambra: A Chronicle of the Conquest of Granada* in his *Complete Works* (New York: Putnam, 1880-1888).
5. Paine, *Buried Treasure*, p. 16.
6. Cora L. Daniels and C. M. Stevens, *Encyclopedia of Superstitions, Folklore and the Occult Sciences of the World* (Chicago: Yewdale, 1903) p. 731.
7. *The Folk-Lore Journal*, V (1887) p. 30.
8. Cotton Mather, *Magnalia Christi Americana: The Ecclesiastical History of New England from Its First Planting in the Year 1620 Unto the Year of Our Lord 1698* (Hartford: Andru, 1855).
9. Adolphe F. Bandelier, *The Gilded Man*, (New York: n.p., 1893) p. 26.
10. Bandelier, *Gilded Man*, p. 19.
11. Paine, *Buried Treasure*, pp. 3-35, 240 ff. Paine has a good collection of pirate stories. He gives definite directions for finding the Cape Vidal, Jamaica, Madagascar, Phillipine, Lafitte (Gulf of Mexico), Captain Kidd (Atlantic seaboard), Cocos Island, Guam, Vladivostok, Clipperton Island, Gallapagos, Straits of Magellan, Madeira, Trinidad and other treasures.
12. J. Frank Dobie, *Legends of Texas*, Publication of the Texas Folk-Lore Society, No. 3 (Austin, TX: Folk-Lore, 1924) ,pp. 29,32, 34, 41, 50, 52, 80, 82, 87, 07.
13. Charles M. Skinner, *Myths and Legends Beyond Our Borders* (Philadelphia: Lippincott, 1899) p.68.

IOWA LEGENDS OF BURIED TREASURE

14. Paine, *Buried Treasure*, pp. 35-41.
15. H. A. Guerber, *Legends of the Rhine* (New York: Barnes, 1899) p. 271.
16. *The Pirate's Own Book* (n.p.: n.p., n.d.) quoted in Paine, *Buried Treasure*, p. 4. "... [A]lthough great treasures lie hid in this way it seldom happens that any is recovered."
17. See Chapter 6 "Black Hawk" and Chapter 40 "Dream Tree."
18. Dobie, *Legends of Texas*, p. 10. Dobie calls attention to the effect of the 1849 rush upon a state having gold. The same movement affected Iowa, but probably not greatly its legends. Returned miners found gold near Steamboat Rock, Anamosa, Graettinger and other points. A few legendary heroes were disappointed prospectors.
19. Dobie, *Legends of Texas*, p. 10, "... [R]ecently (1924) a man was indicted in Fort Worth (Texas) for fraudulently obtaining money on pretense of organizing an expedition to seek $5,000,000 in gold nuggets in a cave in Mexico. How the nuggets got in the cave involved a long story around an Indian, General Custer, Jesse James and Pancho Villa. It was a good story!"
20. Irving, "The Journey," *Complete Works*.
21. Dobie, *Legends of Texas*, p. 11. Dobie also says, "It is as easy to promise gold as it is to promise rain and in a country in which neither is plentiful the Mexican shows his desire to please by predicting both."
22. Paine, *Buried Treasure*, p. 7. George R. Sims, quoted by Paine, "Respectable citizens, tired of the melancholy sameness of a drab existence, cannot take to crepe masks, dark lanterns, silent matches and rope ladders, but they can all be off to a pirate island and search for treasure and return laden or empty and without a stain on their characters." Robert Louis Stevenson supported treasure hunts. [*Essays*, "Eldora-do"]. Benjamin Franklin, however, noted many pits outside Philadelphia and in his Busy-Body Series, quoted "Agricola of Chester County," "My son, I give thee now a valuable parcel of land, I assure thee I have found considerable gold by digging there; thee mayest do the same; but thee must carefully observe this, **Never to dig more than plow deep.**"
23. Dobie, *Legends of Texas*, p. 6. "The Spanish found great wealth in America. They became credulous of mythical wealth. Later ages and folk, failing to inherit their wealth, inherited their credulity."
24. *The Des Moines Register*, 10 Mar. 1927, p. 2. Last March two men were arrested in Chicago on charges of collecting nearly $1,000,000 to exploit a race of pygmies in Columbia. Oil, gold, platinum and precious stones were to be the proceeds and the pygmies were pictured eating from gold vessels.

Endnotes

NOTES TO CHAPTER 1.

25. Bruce E. Mahan, *Old Fort Crawford and the Frontier* (Iowa City, IA: State Historical Society, 1926). The post was originally called Fort McKay, according to Mahan, and was renamed presumably for General Crawford.
26. I believe this to be a typographical error. The inhabitants usually mention either $80,000 or $90,000.
27. Cf. Paine, *Buried Treasure*, p. 357; Walter Johnson, *Folk-Memory, or the Continuity of British Archaeology* (Oxford: University, 1908) p. 164; Letter received from Lena Brady, Sutherland, Iowa, n.d.

NOTES TO CHAPTER CHAPTER 2.

28. Cf. G. W. Weippert, "Legends of Iowa," *Journal of American Folklore*, II, (1889) pp. 287-290; Edward E. Winslow, "Western Mono Myths," *Journal of American Folklore*, XXXVI (1923) p. 366; Sir James George Frazer, *Folk-lore in the Old Testament: Studies in Comparative Religion, Legend and Law* (New York: Macmillan, 1923) 243 ff.; J. Leeper Gay, "The Accursed Gold in the Santa Anna Mountains," in Dobie, *Legends of Texas*, p. 78.
29. Nezeka was probably two miles north, but I here use the version of my informants. See Ellery M. Hancock, *History of Allamakee County and Its People* (Chicago: Clark, 1913) pp. 235-236.
30. Cf. Elizabeth Andrews, *Ulster Folklore* (London: Elliot, 1913) p. 64, 84.; Alanson Skinner, "Plains Cree Tales," *Journal of American Folklore*, XXIX (1916) pp. 341-368.
31. Dousman is an accretion point for legend. He died many times and violently.
32. The Dousman House was for many years the chief stopping point between Dubuque and La Crosse. It was locally considered of sufficient historical interest to be offered to President Calvin Coolidge as a vacation resort for the summer.

NOTES TO CHAPTER 3.

33. Hancock, *History of Allamakee*, pp. 55-61, 233-234.
   According to the treaty of 1832 signed at Rock Island, part of the Winnebagoes were to occupy the neutral ground and the nation was to receive $10,000 a year and a school near Prairie du Chien. The money was to be paid at forts Crawford and Winnebago. The school budget was $3,000 a year. The building was a fine two-story relic a few miles above the mouth of Yellow River. It has now been demolished that the stone might be utilized "for more useful buildings for the present day farmer."

IOWA LEGENDS OF BURIED TREASURE

NOTES TO CHAPTER 5.

34. For an explanation of these, see Realto E. Price, *History of Clayton County, Iowa*, I (Chicago: Law, 1906); "Giard Township," *The Herald*, 12 Mar. 1922, p. 2.
35. Cf. Daniels and Stevens, *Encyclopedia of Superstitions*, III, p. 1664 ff.; Andrew Lang, "The Divining Rod," *Custom and Myth* (New York: Harpers, 1885); F. F. Young and William Roberts, *The Divining Rod and Its Uses* (London: n.p., 1894); Paine, "The Divining Rod," *Buried Treasure*; Abbe Le Lorraine de Vallemont, *La Physique Occulte* (Paris: n.p., 1876); Cyrenus Cole, *History of the People of Iowa* (Cedar Rapids, IA: Torch, 1921) p. 223; Samuel Adams Drake, *Myths and Fables of Today* (Boston: Lee, 1900) p. 232.
36. File No. 314.7/74618 FAA, Apr. 7, 1927.

NOTES TO CHAPTER 6.

37. The essentials of this battle are well established. Mahan, *Old Fort Crawford*, has a good account.
38. Estimates run as high as 300. See Randall Parish, *Historic Illinois* (Chicago: McClurg, 1905) p. 269. Hancock, *History of Allamakee*, pp. 251-252, quotes Capt. E. B. Bascom of Lansing to the effect that Black Hawk himself swam the river and was captured by the Winnebagoes on Brookman's Bluff above New Albin. This is not generally credited and is denied by the victim himself, who claims in his autobiography to have voluntarily given himself up after escaping from the massacre. As to the gold, Black Hawk captured food and munitions in his early victories and plundered sections of Illinois. Some educated and presumably comfortable families were killed, but there is no indication that the Indians acquired more than trinkets and bric-a-brac, if indeed they wanted much of that. See *The Davenport Gazette*, 30 June 1859; Willard Barrows, "The Black Hawk War," *History of Davenport and Scott County* (Chicago: Clark, 1910); E. H. "Timothy" Flint, "Black Hawk," *Indian Wars of the West*; (Cincinnati: n.p., 1833).
39. Cf. Alexander von Humboldt, *Cosmos: A Sketch of a Physical Description of the Universe*, trans. E. C. Otto, I (London: Bell, 1871) p. 1259; Parker Fillmore, "The Flaming Horse," *Czechoslovak Fairy Tales* (New York: Harcourt, 1919); Mariana Montiero, *Legends and Popular Tales of the Basque People* (New York: Armstrong, 1887) pp. 52-79; Daniels and Stevens, II, *Encyclopedia of Superstitions*, p. 731; Charles M. Skinner, *Myths and Legends Beyond Our Land* (Philadelphia: Lippincott, 1900) pp. 68-69; Knut Stjerna, *Essays on Questions Connected with the*

Endnotes

Old English Poem of Beowulf, trans. J. R. Hall (London: Clark, 1912) cited in Bertram Windle, "Reviews," *Folk-Lore,* XXIV (1913) p. 256; *The Folk-Lore Journal,* I (1887) pp. 184-187; Daniel Thomas, Lindsey Blayney and Lucy Blayney, *Kentucky Superstitions* (Princeton, NJ: University, 1920) No. 3949.

NOTES TO CHAPTER 8.

40. H. M. Chittenden, "Report on Steamboat Wrecks in the Missouri River," VIII, *Nebraska History Magazine,* (Dated Jan.-Mar., 1925: printed Feb. 1927) p. 22, mentions sinking of *Mollie Dozier,* a side wheel boat, 225 x 34 feet, "just below Council Bluffs." It would have been one of the large boats of the time and is said to have struck a snag.
41. It may have drifted downstream. I have been told that newspaper articles a few years back reported a hunt for such a barge at Pierre, SD, with great show of machinery. There was an early belief in mines along the Missouri. Chittenden, "Steamboat Wrecks," p. 9 ff.
42. A bend in the river at this point is grave stone to the *Bertram,* the *Benton,* the *Cora II* and the *Amanda.* Chittenden, "Steamboat Wrecks," pp. 20-22.

NOTES TO CHAPTER 9.

43. I find no reference to these events in histories of Jasper and Marshall counties. Bank robberies furnish racy and available copy and are thus usually included.

NOTES TO CHAPTER 10.

44. *The Eddyville Tribune,* 6 Nov. 1903, p. 1. rpt., *The Des Moines Register,* 21 Nov. 1920, p. 1.
45. *The Eddyville Tribune,* p. 1.
46. *The Eddyville Tribune,* 13 Nov. 1903, p. [?]. The issue is actually dated like the previous number.
47. *The Eddyville Tribune,* 13 Nov. 1903, p. [?].
48. This is a sharpened iron rod about 6 feet long, half an inch thick and with a cross rod for hand holds perhaps a foot and a half from the blunt end.
49. *The Des Moines Register,* Nov. 21, 1920, p. [?].

NOTES TO CHAPTER 11.

50. November 14-28, 1920. Newspapers all over the country carried the essential facts. *The Nonpariel,* in Council Bluffs, *The News,*

IOWA LEGENDS OF BURIED TREASURE

The Bee, and the *World-Herald*, in Omaha, covered the case extensively.
51. *The Des Moines Register*, 18 Mar. 1922.
52. *The Evening Tribune*, (Des Moines, IA), 1 Jan. 1925 and 31 Jan. 1925; *The Des Moines Register*, 26 Dec. 1924.
53. *The Evening Tribune*, 31 Jan. 1925.
54. *The Evening Tribune*, 1 Jan. 1925.

NOTES TO CHAPTER 12.

55. Most of the above details can be found in *The Bloomfield Democrat*, 22 Mar. 1917 in what purports to be an interview with W. S. Wallace.
56. Edward Bonney, *The Banditti of the Prairies or the Murderer's Doom* (Chicago: Homewood, 1847) p. 222 and [Editor's footnote]. A. R. Fulton, *The Red Men of Iowa, Being a History of the Various Aboriginal Tribes* (Des Moines, IA: Mills & Company, 1882) pp. 342-349.

NOTES TO CHAPTER 13.

57. Willard Glazier, "Diary of Sept. 8, 1881," *Down the Great River* (Philadelphia: Hubbard, 1893).
58. Cole, *History of the People of Iowa*, p. 161. [Editor's endnote]. For another detailed and slightly different version of the Bellevue War see A. T. Andreas, *Illustrated Historical Atlas of the State of Iowa* (Chicago, IL: Andreas Atlas Co., 1875) p. 444.
59. Benjamin F. Gue, *History of Iowa* (New York: Century Hist., 1903) pp. 332-334.

NOTES TO CHAPTER 14.

60. [Editor's endnote]. Fulton, *The Red Men*, pp. 293-297.

NOTES TO CHAPTER 15.

61. [Editor's endnote]. Fulton, *The Red Men*, pp. 293-297.

NOTES TO CHAPTER 16.

62. Indians are said to have taken $1,000 from Marble's body. Abbie Gardner-Sharp, *The Spirit Lake Massacre* (Des Moines, IA: Homestead, 1918) pp. 66-71, 82 ff. [Editor's endnote]. The murder of Mr. Marble on March 13, 1857, and the kidnapping of his wife are described in Fulton, *The Red Men*, pp. 305-306.

Endnotes

NOTES TO CHAPTER 22.

63. I have found no account of such a holdup or pursuit. The James brothers were popularly reputed to have taken nearly $300,000. J. W. Buel, *The Border Bandits: An Authentic and Thrilling History of the Noted Outlaws Jesse and Frank James and Their Bands of Highwaymen* (Chicago: National, 1893) p. 248.

NOTES TO CHAPTER 24.

64. Homer H. Field and Joseph R. Reed, *History of Pottawattamie County, Iowa*, I (Chicago: Clark, 1907) p. 14.

NOTES TO CHAPTER 26.

65. J. M. Reid, *Sketches and Anecdotes of the Old Settlers and the New Comers: The Mormon Bandits and the Danite Band* (Keokuk: Ogden, 1896) p. 155.

NOTES TO CHAPTER 27.

66. The Rainsbarger story is treated fictionally in Herbert Quick, *The Hawkeye*, (Indianapolis: n.p., n.d.) pp. 435-67. *The Des Moines Register*, 3 Nov. 1903, reflects the traditional point of view. E. C. Moore, *The Des Moines Register*, Magazine Section, 12, 19, 26 Dec. 1926 and 2 Jan. 1927, gives an inaccurate but essentially just account.
67. I am aware that many believe the Rainsbargers innocent if unsocial victims, and that there is reason for the belief. Regardless of historical accuracy, popular sentiment determines legend.

NOTES TO PART 3.

68. *The Des Moines Register*, Magazine Section, 30 Apr. 1926, p. 3.
69. *The Des Moines Register*, 14 Jan. 1927.
70. *The Des Moines Register*, Magazine Section, 16 Jan. 1927.

NOTES TO CHAPTER 39

71. Weston A. Goodspeed, *History of Dubuque County, Iowa* (Chicago: Weston A. Goodspeed, 1912 [?]) p. 19 ff.; Charles R. Tuttle, and Daniel S. Durrie, *History of the State of Iowa, from Its First Explorations Down to 1875* (Chicago: Peale, 1876) p. 25; Horace M. Rebok, *The Last of the Musquaki and the Indian Congress* (Dayton, OH: Funk, 1898) p. 27; [Editor's endnote] Andreas, *Illustrated Historical Atlas*, pp. 423-424.

72. Goodspeed, *History of Dubuque County*, p. 29.

NOTES TO APPENDIX

73. H. J. Rose, "Reviews," *Folk-Lore*, XXV (1914), p. 133, contains a short review of the theory that dragons grow out of the belief that the dead return in snake form. George Henderson in the introduction for J. G. Campbell, *The Celtic Dragon Myth: With the Geste of Fraoch and the Dragon* (Edinborough: Grand, 1911) p. 12 ff. has a discussion. In India is the belief that a serpent made of the flower of Urad pulse wards treasure. *Madras Times*, Dec. 24, 1907, quoted in *Folk-Lore*, XX (1909), p. 211. See also Cannon H. Callaway, *The Religious System of Amazulu* (London: Folk-Lore, 1884) p. 142 and Col. J. Shakespeare, "The Religion of Manipur," *Folk-Lore*, XXIV (1913), p. 422. Many mythologies exceed the Christian, making the serpent the creator.
74. Samuel Adams Drake, *A Book of New England Legends and Folklore in Prose and Poetry* (Boston: n.p., 1883) p. 346. H. J. Rose, "Prentice Pillars," *Folk-Lore*, XXXIV (1924), p. 381. Paine, *Buried Treasure*, pp. 159-70.
75. Nicholas Belfield Dennys, *The Folk-Lore of China and Its Affinities with that of the Aryan and Semitic Races* (London: Trubner, 1876) p. 112.
76. Letter from W. W. Wilford, Greenville, Illinois, n.d.
77. Newbell Niles Puckett, *Folk Beliefs of the Southern Negro* (Chapel Hill, NC: Univ. of NC, 1926) p. 26.
78. Paine, *Buried Treasure*, p. 10.
79. Mary Julie MacCulloch, "Folklore of the Isle of Skye," *Folk-Lore*, XXXIII (1922) p. 386.
80. Davis Rorie, "Stray Notes on the Folk-lore of Aberdeenshire and the Northeast of Scotland," *Folk-Lore*, XXV (1923) p. 234.
81. Charles M. Skinner, *Myths and Legends of Our Own Land*, I (Philadelphia: Lippincott, 1896) pp. 125-127.
82. Paine, *Buried Treasure*, pp. 10-11.
83. Paine, *Buried Treasure*, p. 10.
84. Daniel Thomas, Lindsay Blayney and Lucy Blayney, *Kentucky Superstitions* (Princeton, NJ: University, 1920). Nos. 322, 372, 1085, 1316, 1319, 1355, 2177, 3017-23, 3775, 3800-4, 3829, 3833, 3850, 3881, 3916.
85. Rose, "Prentice Pillars," p. 381.
86. John Philipps Emslie, "Scraps of Folklore Collected by . . . ," *Folk-Lore*, XXVI (1915) pp. 156-157.
87. L. M'Manus, "Folk-Tales from Western Ireland," *Folk-Lore*, XXV (1914), pp. 337-338.
88. John Rhys, *Celtic Folklore, Welsh and Manx*, I (Oxford: Clarendon, 1901) p. 469.

Endnotes

89. Rhys, *Celtic Folklore*, p. 471.
90. Bernard Henderson and C. Calvert, *Modern Tales of Ancient Spain* (London: n.p., 1924) pp. 31-48.
91. Charlotte Sophia Burne, *Shropshire Folk-Lore: a Sheaf of Gleanings* (London: Trubner, 1923) p. 83.
92. B. Hunt, *Folk Tales of Breffny* (London: Macmillan, 1912) p. 181.
93. Daniels and Stevens, *Encyclopedia of Superstitions*, p. 731.
94. Skinner, *Myths and Legends Beyond Our Land*, p. 68.
95. W. H. Jones and L. L. Krope, eds., *Folk Tales of the Magyars* (London: Folk-Lore, 1889) Intro., p. 30.
96. Paine, *Buried Treasure*, p. 10.
97. Paine, *Buried Treasure*, p. 16.
98. Emelyn E. Gardner, "Folk-Lore from Schoharie County, New York," *Journal of American Folk-Lore*, XXVII (1914) p. 323.
99. Thomas Wright, *A History of Caricature and Grotesque* (London: Chatto, 1875) p. 62.
100. Estella Canziani, "Collecteana," *Folk-Lore*, XXIV (1913) p. 363.
101. Paine, *Buried Treasure*, pp. 9, ff. 404.
102. Jones and Kropf, *Folk Tales of the Magyars*, Intro., p. 31, footnote.
103. *Folk-Lore*, Vol. XXI (1910), p. 344.
104. *Journal of American Folklore*, XXXV (1922), p. 290.
105. Jones and Kropf, *Folk Tales of the Magyars*, p. 231.
106. Ella M. Leather, *Folk-Lore of Herefordshire* (London: n.p., 1912) p. 33.
107. C. Richardson, "Some Slave Superstitions," *Southern Workman*, 41 (1912), p. 246.
108. Burne, *Shropshire Folk-Lore*, p. 640.
109. Thomas, Blayney and Blayney, *Kentucky Superstitions*, p. 18.
110. Thomas, Blayney and Blayney, *Kentucky Superstitions*, No. 3088, p. 233.
111. Thomas, Blayney and Blayney, *Kentucky Superstitions*, No. 3416. "Stamping" is defined as counting, emphasizing each unit by wetting one hand with saliva and striking it with the other.
112. e.g., Mother Fox, in Shropshire lore, finds 400 pieces of silver under an alder bush, using this method. See Burne, *Shropshire Folk-Lore*. p. 262.
113. G. F. Abbott, *Macedonian Folklore*, (Cambridge: University, 1903) p. 226, footnote 1.
114. Thomas Frederick Crane, *Italian Popular Tales* (New York: Houghton, 1885) p. 156.
115. Humboldt, *Cosmos*, p. 1259.
116. Fillmore, *Czechoslovak Fairy Tales*.
117. Mariana Monteiro, *Legends and Popular Tales of the Basque People* (New York: Armstrong, 1887) pp. 52-79.
118. Daniels and Stevens, *Encyclopedia of Superstitions*, II, p. 731.
119. Daniels and Stevens, *Encyclopedia of Superstitions*, II, p. 731.

120. Skinner, *Myths and Legends Beyond Our Land*, p. 68.
121. Skinner, *Myths and Legends Beyond Our Land*, p. 69.
122. Knut Stjerna, *Essays on Questions Connected with the Old English Poem of Beowulf*, trans. J. R. Clark Hall. In Bertram Windle, "Reviews," *Folk-Lore*, XXIV (1913) p. 256.
123. *The Folk-Lore Journal*, I (1887) pp. 184-187.
124. Thomas, Blayney and Blayney, *Kentucky Superstitions*. No. 3949.
125. Isabella Augusta Gregor, *Visions and Beliefs in the West of Ireland*, (London: Putnam, 1920) p. 9.
126. Paine, *Buried Treasure*, p. 10.
127. Jones and Kropf, *Folk Tales of the Magyars*, p. 405.
128. Eiriker Magnusson and William Morris, *Grettis Saga, The Story of Grettir the Strong* (London: Ellis, 1869) p. 47.
129. William A. Craigie, *Scandinavian Folk-Lore: Illustrations of the Traditional Beliefs of the Northern Peoples*, trans. Alexander Gardner (London: Gardner, 1896) p. 265.
130. T. M. Dawkins, "Ancient Statues in Medieval Constantinople," *Folk-Lore*, XXXV (1924), p. 243. Professor Dawkins points out that statues are sometimes thought to be demons or men turned to stone to guard treasure. This treasure was located by digging under the finger of a statue.
131. Fannie Ratchford, "Native Treasure Talk Up the Frio," in *The Legends of Texas*: Publications of the Texas Folk-Lore Society, No. 3 (Austin, TX: Folk-Lore, 1924) pp. 57-59.
132. The difficulty of deciding where one treasure stops and another begins precludes an accurate figure.
133. Any collection of Irish fairy tales is full of such treasure. T. Crofton Crocker, *Fairy Legends and Traditions of the South of Ireland* (London: Swan, 1882) is perhaps the best.
134. A Kinnagoe (Ulster) man dreamed he must go to London bridge where a chance passer told him a dream of a pot of gold in Kinnagoe, by which pot the first became rich. Andrews, *Ulster Folklore*, p. 84. Treasure dreams are common.
135. e.g. Andrews, *Ulster Folklore*, p. 64.
136. Skinner, "Plains Cree Tales," *Journal of American Folklore*, p. 357.
137. *The Bible*, Exodus, XVI, 33; XXVII, 2: I. Kings, VI, 25, 26; Samuel II, 13-15; Numbers, XVI, 17, 18; Jeremiah I, 13; Zechariah XIV, 20, 21; Mark, VII, 4.
138. It was, however, an oak that is said to have sprung up recording a miraculous birth and thereby gave a name to Lone Tree, IA, see Weippert, "Legends of Iowa," *Journal of American Folklore*, pp. 287-290.
139. John R. S. S. Aubrey, *Remains of Gentilisme and Judaisme*, ed. James Britten (London: Folk-Lore, 1881) p. 155.

Endnotes

140. Edward E. Winslow. "Western Mono Myths," *Journal of American Folklore*, XXXVI (1923), p. 366.
141. Sir James George Frazer, *Folk-lore in the Old Testament: Studies in Comparative Religion, Legend and Law* (abridged). (New York: n.p., 1923) pp. 243 ff.
142. Helderii Friend, *Flowers and Flower Lore* (London: Swan, 1884) lists some fifty-two of these. See also William George Black, *Folk Medicine: A Chapter in the History of Culture* (London: Folk-Lore, 1883) 37 ff.
143. Jacob Grimm, *Teutonic Mythology*, cited in George Lawrence Gomme, *Folk-Lore Relics of Early Village Life* (London: Stock, 1883) p. 17.
144. Charlotte Sophie Burne, *The Handbook of Folklore* (London: n.p., 1914) p. 31.
145. E. R. Sherrill, "Lost Copper Mines and Spanish Gold, Haskell County," Dobie, *Legends of Texas*, p. 75.
146. J. Leeper Gay, "The Accursed Gold in the Santa Anna Mountains," Dobie, *Legends of Texas*, p. 78.
147. Letter from Mrs. John Wermerson, Britt, IA, n.d.
148. Andrew Lang. *Myth, Ritual and Religion*, I (London: n.p., 1906) p. 125.
149. Paine, *Buried Treasure*, p. 357.
150. Johnson, *Folk-Memory*, p. 164.
151. Skinner, *Myths and Legends of Our Own Land*, Vol. II, p. 13.
152. Gregor, *Visions and Beliefs*, p. 35.
153. Michael Aislabie Denham, *The Denham Tracts*, ed. by James Hardy, II (n.p., 1846-1859, rpt. London: n.p., 1895) p. 202.
154. Denham, *Denham Tracts*, p. 135: 200-202.
155. William Caxton, *The History of Reynard the Fox*, ed. Edward Arbor (Westminster: Constable, 1895) pp. 33 ff.
156. Carl Lumholtz, *Unknown Mexico* (New York: Scribners, 1902) p. 485.
157. Letter from Lena Brady, Sutherland, Iowa, n.d.
158. Ernest Whitney and William S. Alexander, *Legends of the Pike's Peak Region* (Denver: Chain, 1892) p. 15.
159. Daniels and Stevens: *Encyclopedia of Superstitions*, III, p. 1664, ff: Lang, "The Divining Rod," *Custom and Myth;* Young and Roberts, *The Divining Rod and Its Uses*; Paine, "The Divining Rod," *Buried Treasure*: Vallemont, *La Physique Occulte*.
160. Cole, *History of the People of Iowa*, p. 223.
161. Drake, *Myths and Fables of Today*, p. 232.

IOWA LEGENDS OF BURIED TREASURE

Select Bibliography

BOOKS

Abbot, G. F. *Macedonian Folklore*. Cambridge: University, 1903.
Andrews, Elizabeth. *Ulster Folklore*. London: Elliot, 1913.
Aubrey, John R. S. S. *Remains of Gentilisme and Judaisme*. Ed. James Britten. London: Folk-Lore Society, 1881.
Barrows, Willard. *History of Davenport and Scott County*. 2 vols. Chicago: Clark, 1910.
Beckwith, Martha Warren. *Jamaica Anansi Stories*: Memoirs of the American Folk-Lore Society, No. [?]. n.p.: Folk-Lore Society, 1924.
Black, William George. *Folk Medicine: A Chapter in the History of Culture*. London: Folk-Lore Society, 1883.
Bleek, William Heinrich Immanuel. *Specimens of Bushman Folklore*. Trans. L. C. Lloyd. Ed. L. C. Lloyd. London: Allen, 1911.
Bonney, Edward. *The Banditti of the Prairies, or The Murderer's Doom*. Chicago: Homewood, 1847.
Brand, John. *Brand's Popular Antiquities of Great Britain*. London: Reeves, 1905.
Brinton, Daniel G. *Myths of the New World*. New York: McKay, 1876.
Buel, J. W. *The Border Bandits; An Authentic and Thrilling History of the Noted Outlaws Jessie and Frank James and Their Bands of Highwaymen*. Chicago: National, 1893.
Burne, Charlotte Sophia. *The Handbook of Folklore*. London: Folk-Lore Society, 1914.
----------. *Shropshire Folk-Lore: A Sheaf of Gleanings*. London: Trubner, 1883.
Callaway, Canon H. *Religious System of the Amazulu*. London: Folk-Lore Society, 1884.
Campbell, J. G. *Superstitions of the Highlands and Islands of Scotland*. Glasgow, Scotland: Mac Lehose, 1900.
----------. *The Celtic Dragon Myth: With the Geste of Fraoch and the Dragon*. Edinburgh, Scotland: Grand, 1911.
Caxton, William. *The History of Reynard the Fox*. Ed. Edward Arber. Westminister: Constable, 1895.
Chatelain, Heli. *Folk Tales of Angola*. Memoirs of the American Folk-Lore Society, No. [?]. Boston: Houghton, 1894.
Cole, Cyrenus. *History of the People of Iowa*. Cedar Rapids, IA: Torch, 1921.

IOWA LEGENDS OF BURIED TREASURE

Craigie, William A. *Scandinavian Folk-Lore: Illustrations of the Traditional Beliefs of the Northern Peoples.* Trans. Alexander Gardner. London: Gardner, 1896.
Crane, Thomas Frederick. *Italian Popular Tales.* New York: Houghton, 1885.
Crocker, T. Crofton. *Fairy Legends and Traditions of the South of Ireland.* London: Swan, 1882.
Dake, Orsanus Charles. *Nebraska Legends and Poems.* New York: Pott, 1871.
Daniels, Cora Linn and C. M. Stevens. *Encyclopedia of Superstitions, Folklore and the Occult Sciences of the World.* 3 vols. Chicago: Yewdale, 1903.
Dennys, Nicholas Belfield. *The Folk-lore of China and Its Affinities with that of the Aryan and Semitic Races.* London: Trubner, 1876.
Dobie, J. Frank. *Legends of Texas.* Publications of the Texas Folk-Lore Society, No. 3. Austin, TX: Folk-Lore, 1924.
Drake, Samuel Adams. *Myths and Fables of Today.* Boston: Lee, 1900.
Dyer, Thomas Firminger Thiselton. *Folkore of Women as Illustrated by Legendary and Traditionary Tales, etc.* London: Stock, 1905.
Esquemeling, John. *The Buccaneers of America.* London, Swan, 1910.
Field, Homer R. and Joseph R. Reed. *History of Pottawattamie County, Iowa.* 2 vols. Chicago: Clark 1907.
Fillmore, Parker. *Czechoclavak Fairy Tales.* New York: Harcourt, 1919.
Flint, E. H. *Indian Wars of the West.* Cincinnati, n.p., 1833.
----------. *History of Fremont County, Iowa.* Des Moines, IA: Iowa Historical, 1881.
Fortier, Alcee. *Louisiana Folk Tales in French Dialect and English Translation.* Memoirs of the American Folk-Lore Society, No. [?]. New York: Folk-Lore Society, 1895.
Frazer, Sir James George. *Folk-lore in the Old Testament: Studies in Comparative Religion, Legend and Law.* Abridged. New York: Macmillan, 1923.
----------. Golden Bough: *A Study in Magic and Religion.* 12 vols. London: Macmillan, 1907-1915.
Friend, Helderii. *Flowers and Flower Lore.* 2 vols. London: Swan, 1884.
Fulton, Ambrose Cowperthwaite. *A Life Voyage: A Diary of a Sailor on Sea and Land, Jotted Down During a Seventy-year's Voyage.* New York: Ambrose Cowperthwaite Fulton, 1898.
Fulton, A. R. *The Red Men of Iowa, Being a History of the Various Aboriginal Tribes.* Des Moines, IA: Mills and Company, 1882.
Gardner-Sharp, Abbie. *The Spirit Lake Massacre.* Des Moines, IA: Homestead, 1918.
Glazier, Willard. *Down the Great River.* Philadelphia: Hubbard, 1893.

Select Bibliography

Gomme, George Lawrence. *Folk-Lore Relics of Early Village Life*. London: Stock, 1883.

----------. *Handbook of Folklore*. London: Folk-Lore Society, 1887.

Goodspeed, Weston Arthur and Kenneth Carnell. *History of Dubuque County, Iowa*. Chicago: Weston Arthur Goodspeed, 1912[?].

Gould, E. W. *Fifty Years on the Mississippi*. St. Louis: Nixon, 1889.

Gregor, Isabella Augusta (Perse). *Visions and Beliefs in the West of Ireland*. 2 vols. London: Putnam, 1920.

Gue, Benjamin F. *History of Iowa From Its Earliest Times to the Twentieth Century*. 4 vols. New York: Century History Co., 1903.

Guerber, H. A. *Legends of the Rhine*. New York: Barnes, 1899.

Hancock, Ellery M. *History of Allamakee County and Its People*. Chicago: Clark, 1913.

Hardy, James. *The Denham Tracts: A Collections of Folklore by Michael Aislabie Denham*. 2 vols. London: Folk-Lore Society, 1891-1895.

Hermann, Richard. *Life and Adventures of Julien Dubuque*. n.p.: Dubuque, Settlers' Association, 1906.

----------. *The History of Humboldt County With a History of Iowa*. Cedar Rapids, IA: Historical, 1901.

----------. *History of Hardin County*. 2 vols. Springfield, IL: Union, 1883.

----------. *History of the Counties of Woodbury and Plymouth*. 2 vols. Chicago: Warner, 1890-1891.

----------. *History of Monona County, Iowa*. Chicago: National, 1890.

----------. *History of Marion County*. 2 vols. Des Moines, Union, 1881.

----------. *History of Linn County, Iowa*. 2 vols. Chicago, Western, 1878.

Home, M. P. M. *Mamma's Black Nurse Stories: West India Folk-lore*. Edinborough, Scotland: Blackwood, 1890.

Hopewell, M. *Legends of the Missouri and Mississippi*. London: Ward, 186[?].

Humboldt, Alexander. *Cosmos: A Sketch of a Physical Description of the Universe*. Ed.[?] E. C. Otte. 5 vols. London: Bell, 1871.

Hunt, B. *Folk Tales of Breffny*. London: Macmillan, 1912.

Ingoldsby, Thomas. *The Ingoldsby Legends, or Mirth and Marvels*. London: Bentley, 1891.

Irving, Washington. "The Alhambra, A Chronicle of the Conquest of Granada." In *Complete Works*. New York: Putnam, 1880-1888.

Jacobs, Joseph and Alfred Nutt. *International Folk Lore Congress*. London: Nutt, 1892.

Janvier, Thomas A. *Legends of the City of Mexico*. New York: Harper, 1910.

Johnson, Walter. *Folk-Memory, or the Continuity of British Archaeology*. Oxford: University, 1908.

IOWA LEGENDS OF BURIED TREASURE

Jones, W. H. and L. L. Kropf, Eds. *Folk Tales of the Magyars*. London: Folk-Lore Society, 1889.
Jones, William. *Credulities Past and Present*. London: Chatto, 1898.
Joutell, Monsieur. *A Journal of the Last Voyage Performed by Mons. de la Sale to the Gulph of Mexica, to find out the Mouth of the Mississippi River*. Paris, 1713, London, 1714; rpt. Chicago: Caxton, 1896.
Lang, Andrew. *Custom and Myth*. New York: Harpers, 1885.
Langworthy, Lucius. *Dubuque, Its History, Mines, Indian Legends, etc*. Dubuque, IA: Lit. Inst., 1855.
Larminie, William. *West Irish Folk Tales and Romances*. London: Stock, 1893.
Leather, Ella M. *Folk-Lore of Herefordshire*. London, n.p., 1912.
Lloyd, James F. *Lloyd's Steamboat Directory and Disasters on the Western Waters*. Cincinnati: James F. Lloyd, 1856.
Lorimer, E. L. R. and E. O. Lorimer. *Persian Tales*. London: Macmillan, 1919.
Lumholtz, Carl. *Unknown Mexico*. New York: Scribners, 1902.
MacCulloch, J. A. *The Childhood of Fiction: A Study of Folk Tales and Primitive Thought*. London: Murray, 1905.
MacDougall, James. *Folk Tales and Fairy Lore in Gaelic and English*. Ed. George Calder. Edinburgh, Scotland: Grant, 1910.
Magnus, L. A. *The Heroic Ballads of Russia*. London: Kegan, 1921.
Magnusson, Eiriker and William Morris. *Grettis Saga: The Story of Grettir the Strong*. London: Ellis, 1869.
Mahan, Bruce E.. *Old Fort Crawford and the Frontier*. Iowa City, IA: St. Hist., 1926.
Mather, Cotton. *Magnalia Christi Americana: The Ecclesiastical History of New England: From Its First Planting in the Year 1620, Unto the Year of Our Lord 1698*. 2 vols. Harford: Andru, 1855.
Merrick, George Byron. *Old Times on the Mississippi*. Cleveland: Clark, 1909.
Montiero, Mariana. *Legends and Popular Tales of the Basque People*. New York: Armstrong, 1887.
Paine, Ralph Delahaye. *The Book of Buried Treasure*. New York: Sturgis, 1911.
Parish, Randall. *Historic Illinois*. Chicago: McClurg, 1905.
Parsons, Elsie Clews. *Folk-Lore of the Sea Islands, South Carolina*. Memoirs of the American Folk-Lore Society, No. [?]. New York: Folk-Lore, 1923.
Perrot, Nicolas. *The Indian Tribes of the Upper Mississippi Valley and the Region of the Great Lakes*. Trans. Emma Helen. 2 vols. Cleveland: Clark, 1912.
Prescott, William Hickling. *Conquest of Mexico*. 3 vols. Philadelphia: n.p., 1871.

Select Bibliography

Price, Realto E. *History of Clayton County, Iowa.* 2 vols. Chicago: Law, 1906.

Puckett, Newbell Niles. *Folk Beliefs of the Southern Negro.* Chapell Hill, NC: Univ. of NC, 1926.

Rebok, Horace M. *The Last of the Musquakie and the Indian Congress.* Dayton: Funk, 1898.

Reid, M. M. *Sketches and Anecdotes of the Old Settlers and New Comers: The Mormon Bandits and the Danite Band.* Keokuk, IA: Ogden, 1896.

Rheim, Von Geza. *Drachen und Drachenkampfer.* Berlin, Germany: Ungarn, 1912.

Rhys, John. *Celtic Folklore: Welsh and Manx.* 2 vols. Oxford: Clarendon, 1901.

Sawyer, W. C. *Teutonic Legends in the Nibelungen Lied.* Philadelphia: Lippincott, 1904.

Saxo Grammaticus. *First Nine Books of Danish History.* Trans. Oliver Elton. London: Folk-Lore Society, 1893.

Skinner, Charles M. *Myths and Legends Beyond Our Borders.* Philadelphia: Lippincott, 1899.

----------. *Myths and Legends Beyond Our Land.* Philadelphia: Lippincott, 1900.

----------. *Myths and Legends of Our New Possessions.* Philadelphia: Lippincott, 1902.

----------. *Myths and Legends of Our Own Land.* 2 vols. Philadelphia: Lippincott, 1896.

Stroebe, Clara. *The Swedish Fairy Book.* Trans. Frederick H. Martins. New York: Stokes, 1921.

Teakle, Thomas. *The Spirit Lake Massacre.* Iowa City, IA: St. Hist., 1918.

Thomas, Daniel, Lindsey Blayney and Lucy Blayney. *Kentucky Superstitions.* Princeton, NJ: University, 1920.

Thomas, N. W. *Bibliography of Anthropology and Folk Lore.* London: Nutt, 1908.

Tuttle, Charles R., and Daniel S. Durrie. *History of the State of Iowa, from Its First Exploration Down to 1875.* Chicago: Peale, 1876.

Weaver, Gen. James B. *Past and Present of Jasper County, Iowa.* 2 vols. Indianapolis: Bowen, 1912.

Whitney, Ernest and William S. Alexander. *Legends of the Pikes Peak Region.* Denver, CO: Chain, 1892.

Wilde, Lady (Speranza). *Ancient Legends, Mystic Charms and Superstitions of Ireland.* 2 vols. London: Ward, 1887.

Wright, John W. *History of Marion County, Iowa and Its People.* 2 vols. Chicago: Clark, 1915.

Wright, Thomas. "A History of Caricature and Grotesque." In *Literature and Art.* London: Chatto, 1875.

IOWA LEGENDS OF BURIED TREASURE

Yeats, William Butler. *Irish Fairy and Folk Tales.* New York: Boni, 1918.
Young, F. F. and William Roberts. *The Divining Rod and Its Uses.* London, n.p., 1894.

ARTICLES

Canziani, Estella. "Collecteana." *Folk-Lore,* XXIV (Sep. 1913), 363-365.
Chittenden, H. M. "Report on Steamboat Wrecks in the Missouri River." *Nebraska History Magazine,* VIII (Dated Jan.-Mar., 1925: printed Feb. 1927), 20-26.
Dawkins, R. M. "Ancient Statues in Medieval Constantinople." *Folk-Lore,* XXV (Sep. 1924), 241-256.
Emslie, John Philipps. "Scraps of Folklore Collected by ---." *Folk-Lore,* XXVI (Jun. 1915), 156-157.
Gardner, Emelyn E. "Folk-Lore from Schoharie County, New York." *Journal of American Folk-Lore,* XXVII (Jul. 1914), 304-325.
Gerish, W. B. "Notes and Queries." *Folk-Lore,* I (Sep. 1890), 306.
M'Manus, L. "Folk Tales from Western Ireland." *Folk-Lore,* XXV (Sep. 1914), 337-338.
Rorie, Davis. "Stray Notes on the Folk-lore of Aberdeenshire and the Northeast of Scotland." *Folk-Lore,* XXIV (Dec. 1923), 378-386.
Shakespear, J. "The Religion of Manipur." *Folk-Lore,* XXIV (Dec. 1913) 416-434.
Skinner, Alanson. "Plains Cree Tales." *Journal of American Folk-Lore,* XXIX (Jul.-Sep. 1916), 341-368.
Speck, F. G. "Some Micmac Tales From Cape Breton Islands." *Journal of American Folk-Lore,* XXVIII (Jan. 1915), 59-70.
Williams, Frederick Wells. "Chinese Folklore and Some Western Analogies." Smithsonian Institute, *Annual Report,* No. [?] (1900), 575-600.
Windle, Bertram C. A. "Review." Rev. of *Essays on Questions Connected with the Old English Poem of Beowulf,* by Knut Stjerna. Trans. J. R. Hall. *Folk-Lore,* XXIV (Jul. 1913), 256.

NEWSPAPERS

Bloomfield, IA. *The Bloomfield Democrat,* 22 Mar. 1917.
Davenport, IA. *The Davenport Gazette,* 3 Jun. 1859.
Des Moines, IA. *The Des Moines Register,* 2 Nov. 1903; 16, 21 Nov. 1920; 4 Dec. 1920; 18 Mar. 1922; 16 Dec. 1924; 14, 16 Jan. 1927; 13 Mar. 1927.
Des Moines, IA. *The Evening Tribune,* 1, 31 Jan. 1925.
Des Moines, IA. *The Register and Leader,* 9 Apr. 1905.

Select Bibliography

Dubuque, IA. *The Herald*, 12 Mar. 1922.
Dubuque, IA., *The Telegraph-Herald,* 1 Aug. 1906; 29 Apr. 1917.
Dubuque, IA, *The Times-Journal*, Apr. 29, 1917.
Eddyville, IA. *The Eddyville Tribune*, 30 Oct. 1903; 6, 13 Nov. 1903.
Eldora, IA., *The Ledger*, 6 Apr. 1887.
McGregor, IA, *The North Iowa Times*, 30 Jul. 1905; 25 Jan. 1912.

IOWA LEGENDS OF BURIED TREASURE

Index of Names

A

Adair xi
Adel 79
Aheurn
 John J. 102
Aikins
 Ethan 97
Akins
 Ruby 63, 69
Algona xi, 105
Allamakee
 Co. 23, 31
American Boy 14
Ames xi
 Ben 82
Anamosa xi, 57
 Horse Thief Cave 57
Andrew xi, 33, 35
Anglesey 140
Aquilar
 Don Alonzo de 1
Arguiduna 138
Arkansas 47
Atahaulpa 2
Atkinson
 Fort xii, 13, 15, 27, 28, 141
 General 31
Atlantic xi

B

Bad Ax Bend 31
Badlands 44
Banditti of the Prairies 9, 57
Barnes
 Jack 65
Bartlett 82, 88
Basque 138
Battle Island 31
Beaver
 River 3
Bedouin 136
Bellevue xi, 54, 55, 57, 58, 69
 City Well 59, 61
 War 57, 58, 59, 61
Bence
 Captain 53
Beowulf 138
Bickel
 Daniel 28
 Willie 28
 Willis 16
Bidwell
 Frank 125, 126
 George 125
 Tom "Rags" 125, 126, 127
Birch 54
Black Hawk 9, 31, 32, 139, 141
 War 4, 10
Blomidon 138
Bloody Run
 River 66
Bloomfield 53
Boabdilla
 Governor 2
Boardmann 25
Bohemia 138
Bonaparte 131
Boone 65
 River 63
Bowlder
 Miss 16
Bowman
 Benjamin 97
Braummeier
 Mrs. Harold 73, 74
Breffny 136
Brood
 Wilbur 71
Brookman
 Laura Lou xiii
Brown
 Mrs. R.L. 14
 W.W. 57, 58, 59, 60
 gang 58
 Mrs. 59, 60
Brush Creek 35, 77, 119
 School 77

IOWA LEGENDS OF BURIED TREASURE

Bunker 97
Burns 140
Burton 14
Bury's Ditch
   Shropshire 137
Buxtom 23, 24, 25

C

California 25, 61, 126, 131
Campbell
   Joey 82
Canada
   St. Maurice River 138
Cardona
   Spain 136
Carney
   Charlie 23, 24
   Mrs. 23, 25
   Mary 25
   Ted 23
Carroll
   Co. 115
Cave 69, 74
   Horse Thief 57
   Maquoketa 57
   Robbers' 25
   Treasure Cave 16
Cedar
   River 95
Cedar Rapids xi, 95
Central America 136
Charlie 132, 133
Chetsey
   Surrey 140
Chihuahua 136
China 135
Civil War 4, 39, 111
Claireaux 2
Clayton
   Co. 2, 13, 23
Clovis 1
Clurichauns 139
Cogley
   Doctor 105
Collins

Keith 49, 50
Colorado 20
Columbia
   Lake Quatavita 140
Columbus
   Christopher 138
Confederates 59
Constantinople 138
Cora 141
Cornwall 138
Cottage Grove Place 113
Council Bluffs xi, 37, 49, 75, 82, 84
   Glenn Avenue 89
   Hanger's Hill 89
   Ocean Wave Saloon 91
   Nonpariel 38
Cowman
   Bill 123
Cox
   Colonel 59, 60
   William 65
Cranall 90
Crawford
   Fort xii, 9, 13, 14, 16, 19, 29, 140, 141
Cree
   Indians 139
Creek
   Brush 35, 119
   Summer 107
Crosson
   Sid 47, 48
Cuppy's Grove 95
Czechoslovakia 138

D

Dave 132, 133
Davenport
   George 54
Davis
   Co. 53, 117
   Mrs. Daniel 17
DeLong
   Henry 90

Index of Names

W.W. 43, 44, 46, 47, 48
Des Moines xi, 5, 37, 49, 65, 77, 97, 107, 113, 115, 117, 119, 127
    Cottage Grove Place 113
    Daily News 46
    Drake Park bank 49
    Register xiii, 67, 105, 109
    River 9, 54, 65, 131, 132
De Witt
    Jack 38, 79, 81, 84
Dickinson
    Co. 65, 67
Dousman
    H.L. 15, 17
Drake 2
    University 37
Dreadnought
    Magyar Jack 137
Dubuque 15, 102, 129
    Co. 15, 129
    Julien 129, 130
Duffield 54
Dunreath xi, 121, 123
Dyer
    Mrs. 113

E

Eddyville xi, 2, 43, 44, 46, 140
Edenville 39, (See also Rhodes)
Edward
    the Confessor 136
Efferding
    Louis 58
El Dorado 2
Eldora xi, 97, 98
Ellis
    James 59
Emmet
    Co. 71
Emporia
    Kansas 140
England

Middleston 140
Erickson
    G. Alfred 102, 103
Estherville 28

F

Farley
    Peter 28, 29
Farmington 108
Fiskins
    Bob 98
Flora
    Charles 40
Forney
    Clarence "Toe-hold" 82, 85, 86, 87, 88
Fort
    Atkinson xii, 13, 15, 27, 28, 141
    Crawford xii, 9, 13, 14, 16, 19, 29, 140, 141
    Pierre 38
Fox 35
    William 54, 58, 60, 61
France 1
Fremont
    Co. 81
French 2, 13, 14

G

Galena
    mines 60
Garnder
    Spence 98
Garner
    Township 75
Gerennius
    Cornwall 1
German 31, 139
Germany 115
    Worms 2
Giard xi, 27, 28
Girard (See Giard)
Goidels 140

IOWA LEGENDS OF BURIED TREASURE

Gore 53
Graham 58
Green Island 36
Grettir the Strong 138
Grimm 140
Griswold 75
Grossman
   Irving 37
Grummins 82, 83
Gunton
   William 2, 44, 45, 48

H

Halfhill 69
Hamilton
   Co. 63
Hardin
   Co. 97
Harl
   Hattie 38, 89
Harlan
   Edgar R. 107
Harman
   Richard 130
Harper
   Bill 95
Harrison
   Co. 37, 79
Hawks
   George 28
Hedrick 111
   Opal Chadwick 111
Hereczvara 136
Herefordshire 137
Herodotus 138
Herschelman
   W.M. 35
Hindu 138
Hispaniola 2
Hitchcock
   Frank 38
Hofberg 138
Honey Creek 79
Hood
   Robin 57

Horse Thief Cave 57
Huff
   Warren 38, 90
Huffman 54
Humble Remonstrance, A
   xii
Humboldt
   Co. 65
Hungary
   Mujmbly Hill 137

I

Ibsen's Brand 136
Illinois 58
   Chicago 38
   Greenville 135
   northwest 31
Inca 1, 2
India 140
   West 135
Indian Trail 35
Indiana 47
Ingham
   Harvey 105
Inkpadutah 65, 67
Iowa xii, 9, 16, 31, 37
   Adair Co.
      Adair xi
   Allamakee Co. 13, 19, 27
      Johnsonport 24, 25
      New Albin xi, 30, 31, 102, 137
      Nezeka 15, 17
      Victory [?] 32
      Waukon xi
      Waukon Junction xi, 13, 14, 19, 23
      Waterville 21
   Boone Co.
      Boone 65
   Carroll Co. 115
      Manning 115
   Cass Co.
      Atlantic xi
      Griswold 75

Index of Names

Cerro Gordo Co.
   Mason City 14
Clayton Co. 2, 13, 27
   Eddyville xi
   Giard xi, 27, 28
   McGregor xi, 9, 14, 15, 16, 17, 19, 23, 27, 28
Dallas Co.
   Adel 79
Davis Co.
   Bloomfield 53
   Pulaski 117
   Troy 53
Dickinson Co. 65, 67
   Spirit Lake xi, 63, 65, 66, 67
Dubuque Co. 15
   Dubuque 102, 129
Emmet Co. 71
   Gruver 71
   Estherville 28
Fremont Co.
   Bartlett 82, 88
   King's Hollow 82
   Riverton 82, 88
   Sidney 85, 88
   Thurman xi, 81, 82
Hamilton Co. 63
   Stratford 63
Hardin Co. 97
   Eldora xi, 97, 98
   Steamboat Rock xi, 97, 98
Harrison Co. 37, 79
   Honey Creek 79
   Logan 102
   Pisgah 75
Humboldt Co.
   Livermore 65
Iowa Co.
   Marengo 53, 98
Jackson Co. 33, 35, 57, 69
   Andrew xi, 35
   Bellevue xi, 54, 55, 57, 58, 69
   Maquoketa xi, 35, 57, 59
Jasper Co.
   Newton 39
Johnson Co.
   Iowa City xi
Jones Co.
   Anamosa xi, 57
Keokuk Co. 111
   Hedrick 111
Kossuth Co. 105
   Algona xi, 105
Linn Co. 95
   Cedar Rapids xi, 95
Marion Co. 77, 93, 119, 121, 123
   Brush Creek 119
   Dunreath xi, 121, 123
   Pleasantville 77
   Red Rock 77, 93
Marshall Co. 39
   Edenville 39
   Rhodes 40
   State Center xi, 39
Montgomery Co.
   Villisca 109
Muscatine Co.
   Wilton Junction 73
Polk Co.
   Des Moines xi, 5, 37, 49, 65, 77, 97, 107, 113, 115, 117, 119, 127
   Prairie Center [?] 126, 127
Pottawattamie Co.
   Council Bluffs xi, 37, 39, 49, 75, 79, 82, 84, 89
   Garner Township 75
   Honey Creek 79
   Weston 75, 76
Story Co.
   Ames xi
      University of 115

IOWA LEGENDS OF BURIED TREASURE

Van Buren Co.
  Bonaparte 131
  Farmington 108
  Rising Sun [?] xi, 125
  Stockport 107, 131,
    137, 139
Wapello Co.
  Eddyville 2, 43, 44,
    46, 140
  Ottumwa 43
Webster Co. 63
Winneshiek Co.
  Fort Atkinson xii, 13,
    15, 27, 28, 41
Woodbury Co.
  Sioux City 37, 38
Iowa City xi
Ipswich 140
Ireland 136, 139
  County Claire
    Teermichrain
      Castle 137
Irving
  Washington 4
Island
  Battle 31
  Green 36
Italy 137

J

Jack the Fire King 49
Jackson
  Co. 35, 57, 69
Jake 20
James
  Frank 4, 79
  Henry xii
  Jesse 79, 81
Japan 135
Jennings
  Fron 15
  Jess 131, 132, 133
  Larry 15, 16
Jesus 138
Jew 138

John 131
  Potato 115, 116
Johnson 66, 99
Johnson's Port (see
  Johnsonport)
Johnsonport 24, 25
Jones
  Emperor 136
Juan
  Don 125

K

K.
  Vera 13, 14 (see
    Waulter Scott)
Kansas
  Emporia 140
  Leavenworth 49
  Pilot Mound 140
Kelly 130
  mines 130
Kentucky 59
Keokuk
  Co. 111
Kiever
  River 4
Kimsey
  Michael R. 82, 83
Kincardinshire 135
King
  Mrs. 76
King Arthur 140
King's Hollow 82, 84
Kis-Borosnyo 136
Kossuth
  Co. 105

L

Lafitte
  Jean 2
Laird
  J. G.
    Mrs. 13

Index of Names

Lake
  Manawa 38
  Quatavita 140
  Spirit xi, 63, 65, 66, 67
Landreth
  Y. 63
Lane
  Wilson C. 107
Lange 140
Langybi 136
Le Hew
  Orley 19
  Orville 19
Leavenworth 49
LeBarge
  Jerome 43, 44, 46
Leprechauns 139
Linn
  Co. 95
Little Folks 14
Livermore 65
Locke (see Lott, Henry)
Logan 102
Long
  John 54
Lott
  Henry 65
  John 63 (see Henry Lott)
    monument 63
Louisiana 108
Luzon 2

M

MacDonald 117
Macedonia 137
MacFadden
  George 126
Maish
  Birl 67
Manning 115
Maquoketa xi, 35
  caverns 57
Marble
  Mr. 67
Marengo 53, 98

Marion
  Co. 77, 93, 119, 121, 123
Marjorie 14
Marquette 9
Marshall
  Co. 39
Mary Lou
  riverboat 38
Mason City 14
McCarthy
  Herm 87, 88
McDonnell 69
McDowell 24
McGowan 25
McGregor xi, 9, 14, 15, 16,
  17, 19, 23, 27, 28
Medgelert
  Wales 136
Medon 141
Melalley 44, 45, 46
Mercierre 10
Mexican
  War 2
Mexico City 141
Meyer 139
  Charlotte Kother 28
Military Road 27
Milwaukee
  Railroad 75
Minnesota 9, 19, 79, 88, 126
  Northfield 79
Mississippi
  River 2, 3, 4, 9, 14, 25, 54,
    129
Missouri 9, 53
  River xii, 37, 49, 84
  Saint Louis 38
Mono
  Indians 140
Montana 86
Montgomery
  Co. 109
Moore
  E. C. 109
Moors 1, 4

Morey
  L.S. 29
Mormon 141
Morris
  William 125
Muir
  Baltimore 89, 90
Mujmbly Hill 137
Munsey 14
Murphy
  Donald R. xiii
Muscatine
  Co. 73

N

Nebraska 79
  Omaha 49
New Albin xi, 30, 31, 102, 137
New England 59
New York 97
  Schoharie Co. 136
News, The 46
Nezeka 15, 17
Niagara
  River 2
Nibelungs 2
Nickolson
  Billy 19
North Iowa Times 10
North Skunk
  River 39, 40
Nova Scotia
  Oak Island 2

O

O'Grady
  Michael 101
O'Neill
  Eugene 136
Oak Island 2
Ocean Wave Saloon 91
Oklahoma 141
  Oklahoma City 87

Oldham
  Bobbie 48
Omaha 49
Ottumwa 43

P

Pattison
  Beryl 77, 93, 119, 121, 123
Pennsylvania
  Pittsburg 44, 46
Peru 2
Pictorial Review 14
Piedmont 137
Pierre
  Fort 38
Pike 27
Pike's Peak 9, 141
Pilot Mount 140
Piper
  Edwin Fort xiii
Pisgah 75
Pittsburg 44, 47
Pleasantville 77
Poffenbarger
  Fred 49
Point Anne 16
Polk
  Co. 113, 125
Pottawattamie
  Co. 37, 49, 75, 79, 89
Prairie Center 126, 127
Prairie du Chien 9, 15, 16, 17, 31, 32
Proudfoot
  Mrs. I.E. 127
Pulaski 117

Q

Quarter Way House 27
Quesada 2

Index of Names

R

Ragan
  J.H. 117
Railroad
  Milwaukee 75
  Rock Island 75
Rainsbarger 98, 99
Raynard the Fox 141
Red Rock 77, 93
Remus
  Uncle 5
Rhodes (See Edenville)
Rising Sun xi, 125
River
  Beaver 3
  Bloody Run 66
  Boone 63
  Brush Creek 77
  Cedar 95
  Des Moines 9, 54, 65, 131, 132
  Kiever 4
  Mississippi 2, 3, 4, 14, 25, 54, 129
  Missouri xii, 37, 49, 84
  Niagara 2
  North Skunk 39, 40
  Skunk 41
  St. Maurice 138
  Tiber 136
  Wisconsin 9
  Yellow 13, 14, 19
Riverton 82, 88
Roberts
  Floyd 40
  Hiram 96
Rock Island
  Railroad 75

S

Sac 35
Samuels 89
Santa Anna 140
Santa Fe
  Trail 132
Saskatchewan 139
Scair-nail Dutchy (see George Scholtz)
Scandinavia 138
Schaub
  Mrs. 60, 61
Schneider
  Lena 49
Schoharie
  Co. 136
Scholtz
  George (see Scair-nail Dutchy) 129
Scott
  Waulter (see Mrs. Vera K.) 13, 14
Selkirkshire
  Tamlenchar Cross 140
Servius
  Emperor 138
Shafer
  Joseph 16
Sharp
  Abbie Gardner 67
Shepperd
  Osgood 95
Shinn
  Deacon 90
Shropshire
  Bury's Ditch 137
Sidney 85, 88
Sidominadotah 65
Silvester
  Pope 138
Sinn
  Elizabeth 115
Sioux 35, 65
  City 37
Sixteen 19, 20
Skee 108
Skeeters
  Bill 141
Skunk River 41
Skye
  Isle of 135

171

Smith 38, 58, 141
   R.A. 67
Smithers
   Adelaide 60, 61
Snow
   Mrs. Joseph 44, 47
Snyder
   Mrs. 76
Solomon 136
South Dakota 44
Spain 1, 4, 130
   Cardona 136
Spanish Grant 27
Spirit Lake xi, 63, 65, 66, 67
   massacre 4, 63, 66
Spurlock 96
State Center xi, 39
steamboat
   Warrior 31
Steamboat Rock xi, 97, 98
Steel
   John 48
Stevenson
   Robert Louis xii
Still
   C.M. 131
Stockport 107, 131, 137, 139
Stokesay 136
Stone
   Wilbert 95
Stratford 63
Study
   John 82, 83, 84, 85, 87
Summer
   Creek 107
Swedish 102

T

Tamlenchar Cross
   Selkirkshire 140
Taylor
   Zachary 9, 10
Teermichrain
   Castle 137
Texas 2, 87, 139

Haskell Co. 140
Thurman xi, 81, 82
Tiber
   River 136
Timmerman
   Dora 31
Torrents
   James 82, 83, 84, 87
Trail
   Santa Fe 132
Treasure Island 73
Tribune, The 43, 46
Troy
   bank 53
Two Fingers tribe 65
   Sidominadotah 65
Tye
   Archie 75

U

Uncle Remus 5
Unionist-Copperhead 4
University of Iowa 115

V

Van Buren
   Co. 107, 131
Victory 32
Villisca 109

W

Wabasha 31
Wade
   Martin J. 50
Wagner 2
Wales
   Langybi 136
   Medgelert 136
Wallace
   John 53, 54
   Willie 53
Wallaces' Farmer xi, xiii, 63,
   71, 73, 75, 111, 131

Index of Names

Wapello
  Co. 43
War
  Black Hawk 4
  Civil 4, 39, 111
  Mexican 2
Warren
  Captain 59, 60
  Castle 136
Warrior 31
Washington 14
  Mount. 138
Waterville 21
Waukon xi
  Junction xi, 13, 14, 19, 23
Webster
  Co. 63
Wells
  Polk 82, 88
Westby
  Gordon 53
Weston 75, 76
White
  John 39, 40
Wichita
  Mountains 141
Wick
  Barthinius L. 95
Wickham
  Dad 98
Wight
  Isle of 136
Wilson
  Anna 60, 69
Wilton Junction 73
Winekopf
  Theodore 70
Winnebagoes 31
Wisconsin 9, 31, 82
  Prairie du Chien 9, 15, 16, 17, 31, 32
  River 9
  Treasure Cave 16
Worms 2

Wylie
  James 48

X

Y

Yellow River 13, 14, 19, 20

Z